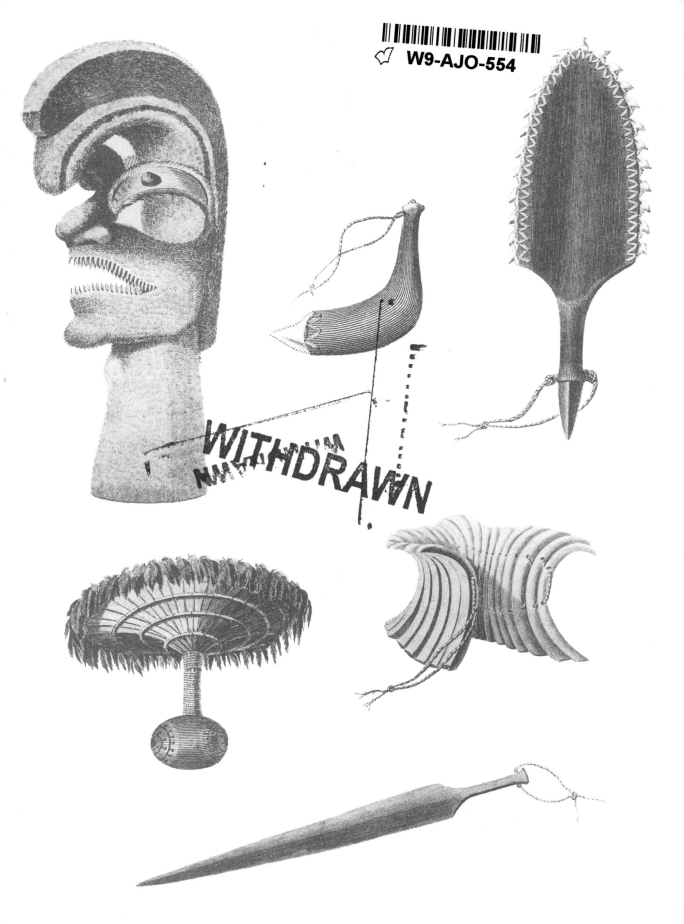

MAGNIFICENT VOYAGE

An American Adventurer

on Captain James Cook's

Final Expedition

MAGNIFICENT VOYAGE

*An American Adventurer
on Captain James Cook's
Final Expedition*

LAURIE LAWLOR

HOLIDAY HOUSE / *New York*

ENDPAPERS: Taken from an engraving
based on expedition artist John Webber's original sketches,
featuring Hawaiian artifacts including a mask, rattles, horns, and a dagger,
from *A Voyage to the Pacific Ocean*, courtesy of Charles Deering McCormick Library
of Special Collections, Northwestern University, Evanston, Illinois.

Library of Congress Cataloging-in-Publication Data
Lawlor, Laurie.
Magnificent voyage: An American adventurer
on Captain James Cook's final voyage /
by Laurie Lawlor.—1st. ed.
p. cm.
Summary: Based on the writings of John Ledyard, an American on the ship *Resolution*,
tells of explorer James Cook's final voyage in search of the Northwest Passage,
discovery of the Hawaiian Islands, and murder.
ISBN 0-8234-1575-9
1. Ledyard, John, 1751–1789—Juvenile literature.
2. Travelers—United States—Biography—Juvenile literature.
3. Cook, James, 1728–1779—Juvenile literature.
4. Voyages around the world—Juvenile literature.
5. Oceania—Discovery and exploration—Juvenile literature.
6. Resolution (ship)—Juvenile literature.
[1. Ledyard, John, 1751–1789. 2. Travelers. 3. Cook, James, 1728–1779.
4. Voyages around the world. 5. Oceania—Discovery and exploration.
6. Resolution (ship) I. Title
G226L5 L38 2002
910'.92—dc21   2002017148

For Jack

"*. . . Behold me the greatest traveller in history, exccentric, irregular, rapid, unaccountable, curious, & without vanity, majestic as a comet . . .*"

—John Ledyard, June 1788, London

CONTENTS

AUTHOR'S NOTE

Writers often invented their own spelling in the eighteenth century. As a result, the spelling and punctuation in the original diaries, logs, and letters used in *Magnificent Voyage* are often very fanciful. Some of the worst spellers were often the best-educated journal keepers. I have tried as much as possible to preserve the original spelling and capitalization in quoted material in order not to change the meaning to fit twenty-first-century grammatical standards.

The explorers' description of indigenous people as "natives" and many of their perceptions about aboriginal groups reflect the attitudes of their time. Without reliable interpreters, gathering information about different cultures was often a difficult, subjective task. My intention is to provide the reader with something of the sense of firsthand discovery Ledyard and the rest of the crew experienced on this amazing journey.

PAINTED BY Wᵐ HODGES.   ENGRAVED BY J. BASIRE 1777

CAPTAIN JAMES COOK. F.R.S.

Captain James Cook's portrait, published in the 1784 edition of A Voyage to the Pacific Ocean *and based on a painting created by William Hodges, official artist of Cook's second round-the-world expedition (1772–1775)*

INTRODUCTION

When Captain James Cook set out in 1776 on a secret mission to discover the elusive Northwest Passage, few would have ever predicted that the voyage would end in tragedy.

To his contemporaries, Cook seemed almost superhuman. At age forty-seven, he was a world-famous celebrity who had traveled farther and mapped more of the Pacific than any other European in the previous 250 years. His ships on two earlier expeditions had returned with scientific data about exotic lands, people, plants, and animals that dazzled Europe and the rest of the world. His expedition journals had been published in heavily illustrated, leather-bound volumes.

In 1776 Cook's accomplishments were the talk of coffeehouses and taverns, literary salons and scientific societies alike. English lords announced Cook's arrival at dinner parties with seventeen-gun salutes. Famous gentlemen wined and dined him in grand style. Cook was presented to King George III and promoted to post captain with a handsome salary. He was awarded the prestigious Sir Godfrey Copley's Gold Medal for his report on maintaining shipboard health. He was elected Fellow of the Royal Society, the highest scientific honor in England. Newspapers sang his praises. Poets celebrated his bravery. He had his official portrait painted. Copies of his image appeared on everything from wallpaper to teapots.

Captain James Cook was a national hero—an intrepid explorer who had successfully ventured where no European had gone before.

In January 1780, three and a half years after Cook had triumphantly departed on his third voyage, the *London Gazette* printed shocking news of the expedition's fate. When King George read the article, he shed tears. The king, like everyone else in England, wanted to believe that the mission had failed because of "barbarian treachery" or natural disaster—not British error or the rash actions of James Cook, who would then be shown to be imperfect and human after all.

As years passed, British books, paintings, speeches, and poems about the last expedition made Cook into a kind of martyr. He was eulogized as a hero who had sacrificed his life to save his crew. Songs, plays, books, poems, paintings, and statues celebrated Cook, the resolute "civilizing" mariner. He became a kind of icon for the British Empire as it expanded into the Pacific.

What really happened on Cook's last voyage?

Fortunately, numerous officers and sailors kept journals during the expedition. Among those whose accounts survive was a relatively unknown young American named John Ledyard. He was an eyewitness—a prickly, critical twenty-four-year-old marine serving with Cook on the *Resolution*.

Ledyard saw what happened. He participated in both the triumphs and tragedies of the four-year voyage. Later, he had the audacity to write and publish his version of the journey in America before the official account from the British Admiralty was released to the public. It's little wonder that the British government and many Cook biographers found Ledyard's best-seller irritating.

This is John Ledyard's story. He speaks to us in a youthful, enthusiastic, irreverent voice that is both wise and foolish, wary and distracted, innocent and jaded, observant and neglectful. He provides us with another view of a mission that was doomed from the start because it was based on so many faulty premises: that seawater could not freeze, that Captain Cook did not need time to rest or recuperate after two back-to-back journeys, that Cook's luck would never give out, that the latest technology could solve anything, and that the British could mistreat less sophisticated native people and not suffer the consequences.

While the expedition sealed the fate of Captain James Cook, it had other, happier, outcomes for Ledyard. He became one of the first Americans to explore the far reaches of the Pacific, including what are now Alaska and Hawaii. He was among the first Americans to encounter Russians in the northern Pacific and visit Siberia. For Ledyard, the voyage caused a kind of

The Apotheosis of Captain Cook, *from a design by P. J. de Loutherbourg, shows how Cook was glorified after his death. This popular image depicts Cook as he ascends into heaven with angels. Below him is Kealakekua Bay and the* Resolution.

transformation. It changed his life and gave him a dream: to return to North America and cross the continent.

Nothing turned out exactly as Ledyard had hoped. He never succeeded in what he once described as "my passage to glory." And yet his vision—what might be called his obsession—never died.

Ledyard inspired an unlikely friend who kept the dream alive. While in Paris, he met Thomas Jefferson, who was serving as American ambassador to France. Like Ledyard, Jefferson was fascinated by the potential of the western wilderness. Ledyard's bold scheme to span the continent on foot and by canoe fired Jefferson's imagination.

It would not be until nearly two decades after Ledyard's death that his vision came true. As president of the United States, Jefferson spearheaded the Lewis and Clark Expedition. The Corps of Discovery reached the Pacific and explored the Northwest. The expedition's findings changed American history forever—in no small part thanks to the seed of a dream planted so many years earlier by John Ledyard.

"I allot myself a seven years ramble more, altho the past has long since wasted the means I had, & now the Body becomes a substitute for cash, and pays my travelling charges."

—John Ledyard to his cousin Isaac Ledyard,
January 15, 1774,
after leaving home and going to sea

COOK'S THIRD VOYAGE (1776–1780)

Plymouth

EUROPE

ASIA

AFRICA

INDIAN

OCEAN

AUSTRALIA

Cape of Good Hope

TASMANIA

KERGUELEN ISLAND
(RESOLUTION ISLAND)

ARCTIC

OCEAN

GREENLAND

ASIA

NORTH

AMERICA

Kamchatka Peninsula

1779

PACIFIC

VANCOUVER
ISLAND

1778–1779

HAWAIIAN ISLANDS

CHRISTMAS ISLAND

SOUTH

AMERICA

SOCIETY ISLANDS

COOK
ISLANDS

FRIENDLY ISLANDS

OCEAN

NEW ZEALAND

MAGNIFICENT
VOYAGE

*An American Adventurer
on Captain James Cook's
Final Expedition*

Chapter 1

CROSSING THE LINE

From Plymouth to the Equator
July–August 1776

When John Ledyard climbed into his hammock on Saturday, August 10, 1776, he did not suspect any danger. The Atlantic night was clear and serene. The voyage so far had been, he wrote, "a very favorable passage."

After a muggy day under a hazy tropical sky, the gentle northeast evening breeze felt fresh and welcome—perfect sleeping weather aboard the *Resolution*. Sails flapped. The wooden ship creaked and sighed contentedly as it headed south along the western coast of Africa.

Below deck, Ledyard's hammock swung back and forth in the darkness. Packed around him, a dozen other sleeping sailors hung like crowded bats suspended from the five-foot six-inch ceiling. In such cramped space a grown man could not stand upright. Each sailor had a width of only sixteen inches in which to sling his hammock. Pick a good one, experienced seamen had advised Ledyard. A hammock was not only a sailor's bed; it also served as a makeshift coffin for burial at sea.

After nearly a month aboard the *Resolution*, Ledyard was still learning the special rituals, language, customs, and dress in this strange new wooden world. He was getting used to the roar of snoring sailors, the rolling smack of waves against the bow, and the lowing and thumping overhead of cattle penned on deck. He was even growing accustomed to the pungent smells of

The reconstructed portrait of John Ledyard, a lithograph on cardboard, was created by an unknown artist long after Ledyard's death. The only two known portraits, self-portraits Ledyard had painted while he was in Europe, have vanished.

tar, mildewed canvas, wet wood, and cow manure, as well as the odors of 111 other unwashed fellow sailors and of the fetid water that sloshed in the bilge, the rounded lower part of the ship's hull.

Corporal Ledyard of the Royal Marines yawned. He reported to Sergeant Samuel Gibson, a feisty Scotsman in his early twenties. Gibson in turn took orders from a lazy, inexperienced twenty-one-year-old, Irish Second Lieutenant Molesworth Phillips. Tonight there seemed little chance of any military action for the fifteen Royal Marine privates and one drummer under the command of Ledyard and the other corporal, James Thomas.

Like the other Royal Marine officers and the privates who served under him, Ledyard enjoyed a few advantages over the *Resolution*'s able seamen, who were officially members of the Royal Navy. Ledyard and the other marines could not be ordered to climb high into the rigging, where most accidents occurred. Best of all, they did not have to serve on night watch, eight hours of keeping alert lookout on deck.

On this particular August evening, Ledyard looked forward to a full night of uninterrupted slumber. What could possibly go wrong on such a peaceful evening with the most famous navigator and superb seaman of the day, Captain James Cook, at the helm?

The crew of the *Resolution* had every confidence in their captain, even though neither Ledyard nor the others knew their destination. Where they were headed was a secret. The dozen veterans who had traveled with Cook before guessed they were bound for another round-the-globe journey and certain glory. And why not? Cook was considered a captain with abounding good luck. He made remarkable discoveries. Most important for Jack Tar, as the common sailor was called, Cook brought his men back safe and in good health—something few British naval officers of his day could claim. A voyage with Cook was the chance of a lifetime, a step up on the ladder to success.

Corporal Ledyard closed his restless blue-gray eyes and dreamed of his own future greatness. At twenty-four, the young American was filled with large hopes and desperate ambitions. Up until now, he had failed at everything he ever tried: law, the ministry, the merchant navy. This expedition, he decided, was his last best chance to finally make good and impress his disappointed family back in Connecticut and New York. All he needed was the opportunity to do something great and gain the attention of mighty, inscrutable Captain Cook. All he needed was the chance to prove himself a hero.

Ledyard did not look heroic to his fellow marines and sailors. He was, they said, of "middling" height—neither tall nor short. (The average grown man at the time stood just five feet six inches tall.) Like many young men of his day, Ledyard wore his long, pale blond hair tied in back in what was then called a queue but is now called a ponytail. His silvery eyelashes and eyebrows must have appeared nearly invisible. His nose was long and aquiline. His complexion was pinkish, and he was easily sunburned. He had broad shoulders. By all accounts, he was a fairly handsome young man and a bit vain about his looks and clothing.

At this early point in the journey, Corporal Ledyard had certainly not revealed his heroic ambitions to any other sailor aboard the *Resolution*. In an able seaman's way of thinking, a marine was not much better than an ignorant landsman.

The marines were supposed to have been taught how to use a musket so that on land they could serve as armed guards and foot soldiers. In a fight at sea, the marines were to line the rail on the poop deck, fire away, and repel boarders from another ship. Much to Corporal Ledyard's disappointment, there had been very little in the way of action.

Lucky for the *Resolution.*

The marines were still "a drunken, quarrelsome set," according to one navy officer. They were untrained and untested. Neither Ledyard nor the privates who served under him were skilled in marksmanship or marching in formation.

The marines aboard the *Resolution* served as extra hands to help able seamen with heavy lifting and hauling—hoisting casks, bales, and hogsheads. They launched the ship's smaller boats and served as rowers. They manned the pumps, pulled ropes and tackle that controlled the sails, and raised the anchor with the capstan, a wheel-like device turned with handspikes and plenty of muscle.

Ledyard was surrounded by numerous crew members who had been at sea since they were ten or eleven years old. They had spent most of their lives unfurling sails and catching the wind. They understood the intricacies of rope and canvas, the unpredictability of wind and weather.

Because sea life was dangerous, hard work, the *Resolution* crew was young. Accidents and illnesses meant that few men reached old age working in the Royal Navy. The average age aboard the *Resolution* was twenty-five. The youngest recorded crew member was sixteen-year-old Midshipman James Trevenen, one of the "young gentlemen" in training to become commissioned officers. The oldest was able seaman William Watman, forty-four. The majority of the 112 men aboard the *Resolution* were English, with a smattering of Scotsmen, Irishmen, Welshmen, and Germans. Five were born in America.

Traveling with the *Resolution* as her consort, or sister ship, was the naval ship *Discovery.* The *Discovery* crew had seventy Englishmen, Irishmen, Scotsmen, and Welshmen, as well as one Dutchman and three Americans. The Jack Tars on both the *Discovery* and the *Resolution* disliked any change in their regular food, drink, or routine. They could be cruel. They could be sentimental. Most were illiterate, superstitious, and prone to be daredevils.

There were layers of social class and sailor caste aboard ship for Ledyard to learn and observe. With whom could he eat? With whom could he converse freely? Whom should he avoid? Above the mass of "people," as the able seamen were called, were midshipmen, known as "young gentlemen." The sons of wealthy merchants or naval men, these young officers were set apart by birth, economic status, and education. Above them were naval officers with experience and rank, and specialists such as carpenters, sail makers, surgeons, and coopers. Over everyone's heads loomed the absolute authority of the captain, whose word was law.

Ledyard had not served as a marine very long before he realized that it was going to be very difficult for anyone of importance to take notice of him. None of the officers knew his name. He wore the same working "short clothes" aboard ship as the other Jack Tars—a short blue jacket (also called a "bum freezer"), loose canvas breeches, a red waistcoat, and a checked shirt with a handkerchief knotted around his neck.

If anyone cared to listen, the only thing that set Ledyard apart from the rest of the sailors was the way he talked. He spouted poetry, theatrical passages, and philosophy. He knew Greek. He knew Latin. Always eager to share his ideas and knowledge, he had what one fellow voyager called "an ardent disposition." His passion for lofty sentiment and romantic description overflowed into the writing he recorded in the journal he kept on the voyage.

Ledyard's flowery words contrasted with the razor-sharp "rough talk" of the average sailor. Sailors used terse, unmistakable expressions that could be heard and understood above a hard gale. They swore and cursed with colorful oaths. ("You fat-gutted chucklehead!") In regular conversation they were "plain dealers." ("None of your jaw, you swab.")

Except perhaps for Second Lieutenant Phillips, the rest of the marines probably did not know how to read and write. Few Jack Tars were impressed with recitations of Virgil or Homer. What mattered aboard ship was not what a sailor said but what he did. Would Ledyard go the extra mile if another crew member's life depended on it? As yet, no one really knew. Not even Ledyard.

Wind luffed the sails. As Ledyard slept on the evening of August 10, a small island along the coast of Africa hove into view. Bonavista, Captain Cook said.

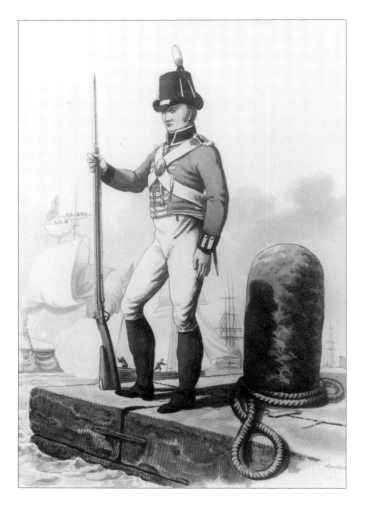

ABOVE:

Watercolor by W. Rowlandson depicting a marine captain in uniform as he would have looked in Ledyard's time

RIGHT:

A common seaman by W. Rowlandson

No one still awake bothered to check the charts. Why take much notice of another dull, familiar island? It had been a languorous, uneventful day in which the most interesting things sighted were porpoises, flying fish, and a sea turtle.

Two hours passed. About eleven o'clock, the *Resolution*'s respected surgeon, William Anderson, came up on deck for some fresh air. As he gazed toward land from the starboard quarter, he heard something in the darkness. The unmistakable crash of breakers.

The ship was headed straight for the rocky shore.

Suddenly, Cook materialized beside Anderson. The powerful six-foot two-inch captain thundered an order to the boatswain. Brown eyes blazing, Cook stared into the darkness.

"Hard astarboard!"

"All hands!"

Instantly, Ledyard and the rest of the sleeping crew awoke. They tumbled out of their hammocks and rushed up the ladder to the deck. Ledyard stumbled into a scene of desperate confusion. If the ship were not instantly turned away from the rocks, it would be dashed to pieces.

"Brace the yards sharp up!"

Sailors scrambled up into the rigging. Ledyard watched in horror as the *Resolution* continued to bear straight ahead. The surf pounded louder and louder. For the next ten minutes, Ledyard could barely breathe. Closer, closer the rocks came. Slowly, painfully, the ship swung around and ran parallel with the shore.

And then the wind died.

Current and waves shoved the ship toward the deadly rocks. For the second time, doom seemed inevitable.

Minutes ticked by. Suddenly, the wind freshened. Sails billowed. The ship steered clear of the breakers. By barely a hair's breadth, they were safe.

Some on board were convinced they owed their lives to Captain Cook's good luck. Others praised his uncanny timing. How else had he appeared on deck, not a moment too late?

Captain Cook himself was characteristically laconic in the notes he made later in his log. "Did but just weather the breakers. Our situation for a few Minutes was very alarming." First Lieutenant John Gore, born in Virginia, always downplayed any crisis. He, too, was subdued. "Saw breakers in our bows" was all he said.

Other officers were more expressive about their horror. Why hadn't Captain Cook noticed the location of the island sooner? And why were they running so close to such dangerous rocks in the dark? Was their great navigator losing his touch?

"To bring a ship into so alarming a situation as we were in at this time without being able to give a satisfactory reason for it certainly deserves the severest reprehension," complained Anderson. The levelheaded twenty-eight-year-old Scotsman couldn't decide if the near miss was due to negligence or complacency—"too accurate a knowledge which often renders us too secure."

Before Ledyard went back to sleep, he heard the accusations. Everyone did. News and gossip traveled fast on such a small ship. Yet it's doubtful Ledyard stayed awake worrying about negligence. In his forever hopeful way of thinking, they had avoided disaster. Wasn't that all that counted?

The next day, however, another embarrassing navigational error was uncovered. They were forty miles off course. The breakers encountered the night before had not been near Bonavista. Cook had misidentified the island—and the danger. Twenty-two-year-old William Bligh, the ship's talented but self-righteous master, was outraged. (He would one day face mutiny aboard the famous *Bounty*, partly because of his own unforgiving nature.) Others were equally disturbed by their captain's navigational error. "I am sure," Anderson grumbled, "no apology can be offer'd for such mistakes as it would seem they are the result of negligence."

Misread maps and a near miss marked the expedition's inauspicious beginning.

The next week passed without further crises. The men fished and recorded visits from puffins, boobies, porpoises, and sharks. Ledyard and the other marines practiced with small arms. They shot off a few cannons. With the rest of the sailors they followed Cook's strict regimen of scrubbing the deck, airing bedding, and smoking the lower deck with special fires. This was Cook's method for warding off disease. "It's always Sunday on Cook's ship," a visiting captain once said. Cook kept an uncommonly clean, orderly ship.

The *Resolution* stood to the southward and made good progress. There was still no sign of the *Discovery,* which was supposed to be hurrying south to meet the *Resolution.* The only way to communicate was to send a written message on a passing ship, a process that might take a month. Captain Cook, who had personally handpicked the *Discovery* captain, Charles Clerke, had no way of knowing that his essential backup ship had not left England until the *Resolution* was at sea for nearly two weeks. Clerke, who had been detained in debtors' prison, was traveling as swiftly as his ship would take them to meet Cook at Table Bay in Africa.

On August 17, herds of porpoises cavorted along both sides of the ship. Storm coming, the superstitious sailors said. Four days later, a large bird settled on the rigging. The strange bird's presence was a bad sign: a "devil's imp" meant to bring mischief.

Soon after, the wind shifted and the rains began in earnest.

And so did the leaks.

During earlier hot, dry weather, gaps had opened between the planking on the ship's sides. The caulk, made from threads of oakum, loose stringy hemp fiber from old rope, and sealed with pitch, fell out. Now the open seams were dangerously exposed.

High waves rolled. Seawater poured into the ship. Rain dripped through the deck and soaked the miserable men below. Bedding turned soggy. Clothing transformed into chafing, sodden armor that never dried. Even officers could not escape the discomfort. To make matters worse, precious extra sails stored in the sail room had become mildewed and ruined by the dampness.

The leaks were caused by shoddy construction back in England. The corrupt Deptford Naval Yards were clearly at fault. Hundreds of ships were being prepared for service in hostilities with the American colonies. War had been officially declared July 4, 1776, with the signing of the Declaration of Independence—just eight days before the *Resolution* left England. It was a boom time for the naval business. Transports crammed with Hessian troops and weapons filled the harbor ready to sail for the colonies.

Unfortunately, preparation and overhauling of the *Resolution* and *Discovery* had not been carefully overseen for this voyage. Captain Cook was too busy with last-minute honors and the editing of his most recent expedition's journals to personally check the work—something he had done on his other two voyages. This oversight would haunt him in the days ahead.

For the next two weeks, intermittent heavy rains plagued the sailors. Waves dashed against the ship. The water was too rough and shark-infested for Cook to send men over the sides on ropes to repair the caulking from the outside. They could only weather the storm and man the pumps. In the meantime, they refilled drinking-water casks with fresh rainwater. "Got three Tuns & a half of rain water," Anderson wrote on August 18.

By September 1, the *Resolution* reached the equator. The rain cleared. The ship hove to and rode steady. That afternoon, with no land in sight, Ledyard was among thirty-five sailors to receive the baptism of "crossing the line." Ledyard was undoubtedly delighted. The initiation rite was one more chance for him to prove his valor. He chose a good ducking over paying the fine—a bottle of rum.

Ledyard straddled a stick tied to a long rope that hung from the yardarm, the outer end of a horizontal length of timber used to spread a sail. Around his waist was attached a line to be used to haul him back again. He held on for dear life as the yardarm swung out over the water. Someone fired a musket and unfurled a flag. The other deep-water sailors, who had already been baptized and were none too sober, gave a cheer. They let go of the rope. Ledyard held his breath and tried his best to land feetfirst to avoid breaking his neck.

Splash! He plunged into the dark water. Down, down, down—until his lungs burned. And when he could hardly hold his breath any longer, he felt himself rising up out of the water into the blinding light. He coughed and hung like a dripping fish on a hook.

"Set him down again!" the sailors shouted.

A proper baptism meant three duckings—sharks or no. Two more times he took the breathtaking plunge, crashed into the sea, and was hoisted out. When he was dumped on deck again, shaking and bedraggled, he was slapped on the back and given a drink of rum. He had passed the test. During the baptism he had borne himself as a brave tar should.

Not everyone aboard the *Resolution* approved of such wild behavior. Crossing the line traditionally meant heavy drinking and dangerous horseplay. Often someone was injured. Anderson, the careful surgeon, wasn't pleased. "The afternoon was spent in the old ridiculous ceremony of ducking those who had not cross'd the Equator before," he wrote. "This is one of those absurd customs which craft and inconsiderate levity has impos'd on mankind and which every sensible person who has it in his power ought to suppress instead of encouraging."

Captain Cook—clearly not acting sensibly enough for Anderson—was resigned to the ancient rite. He had seen it all before. There was no way to avoid the topsy-turvy ceremony in which he himself might be the target of temporary derision.

It's doubtful that Ledyard noticed any friction that the ceremony caused for his superiors. He was too busy enjoying congratulations and toasts from his new watery brotherhood. Now he belonged. For better or worse, he had officially become part of the isolated wooden world of the *Resolution.* There was no turning back. He was a deep-sea sailor now.

Chapter 2

PRIVATEERS AND PROVIDENCE

America
Before 1776

Joining the fraternity of deep-sea sailors must have seemed inevitable for John Ledyard. Salt water ran in his blood. His father, great-grandfather, and uncle had all gone to sea.

His father, Captain John Ledyard, plied the waters of the West Indies in his two-masted square-rigged ship. Captain Ledyard smuggled goods back and forth between Connecticut and the Bahamas—a lucrative business forbidden by England. The British controlled profits and tax revenues by insisting the American colonists trade only with the Mother Country.

Privateers like Captain Ledyard ignored the law. Their ships carried secret cargoes of livestock, wheat, and corn to trade for European hats, cotton stockings, paper, glass, spices, and linen in Caribbean ports like St. Eustatius, the "Emporium of the Caribbean." Nicknamed Money Mountain, this tropical harbor in what is now called the Netherlands Antilles offered anything and everything for sale in a mile-long, double row of warehouses, stores, and slave auction arenas. "Going beyond the line," as privateering in the Caribbean was called, was risky business.

If Captain Ledyard managed to evade other pirates, he faced British and French warship patrols that overtook and boarded any privateers they could catch. And then of course there was the unpredictable Caribbean weather.

November 1751 proved especially dangerous for Connecticut ships in the Caribbean. Early in the month a hurricane hit, overturned a brig, and killed everyone on board except the captain and one crew member. Six local men perished in the storm.

Captain Ledyard, twenty-two, reported no losses. Perhaps because he wasn't at sea.

At home in Groton, Connecticut, his twenty-two-year-old wife, Abigail Hempstead Ledyard, was about to give birth to their first child. Although John Ledyard's exact birthday is unknown, records show that he was baptized November 21, 1751, at Christ Church in Groton. According to custom, he was probably baptized the first Sunday after his birth.

John Ledyard, named for his father, grandfather, and great-grandfather, must have been a hale and hearty baby. In the first two months of his life, four-teen other newborns and young children in the area died—nearly half from an epidemic of "canker," or scarlet fever. And yet John Ledyard survived.

At an early age, John Ledyard learned how to handle small boats on the Thames River, which flowed past his family's home to the sea. From the water's edge, he could readily recognize the difference between brigs, schooners, scows, and shallops. High atop Lantern Hill, overlooking the ocean, he and his beloved younger cousins, Isaac and Ben Ledyard, watched for the first sign of their fathers' ships to return. The two boys were John's constant companions. Their fathers were brothers and business partners.

John Ledyard never spent much time with his father, who was gone for weeks or months at a time. Most of his early memories of his father were snatches of high seas stories embellished with his wild imagination. Captain Ledyard's comings and goings created the rhythm of the household. His current whereabouts, shadowy and exotic, floated in and out of John's consciousness whenever he eavesdropped on his pious mother's nervous conversations. Like so many religious people of her day, Abigail Ledyard believed that anyone who went to sea depended on Providence, the participation of God in human affairs. Everything that happened, she insisted, occurred because of "the workings of God's will."

Providence was not always kind to Captain Ledyard.

In October 1753, when John was almost two years old, a terrible storm carried off the boom and mainsail of Captain Ledyard's ship and washed his cargo of seventeen horses and forty sheep overboard. In 1757 Captain Ledyard's brand-new schooner, named the *Greyhound*, was hijacked by a French ship. A short time later, the *Greyhound* was retaken by a British man-of-war and sailed to Antigua. Captain Ledyard paid a bribe and somehow retrieved the ship but not the cargo.

Five years later, in the spring of 1762, life seemed full of promise for John Ledyard, now nearly eleven years old. Any day now, his mother said, his father was coming home. The long New England winter finally had begun to release its iron grip. Snow melted in the woods outside Groton and the first pale hepatica bloomed. Muskrat tracks crisscrossed thick, pungent mud in nearby Cedar Swamp. Glittering smelt in great spawning runs began their mad dash up the Thames from the Atlantic.

John Ledyard had every reason to feel happy. There were kites to fly, fish to catch, and clattering icy streams and trails to explore with eight-year-old Isaac and seven-year-old Ben.

John wanted for nothing. He lived with his parents, his younger brothers, nine-year-old George and six-year-old Thomas, and sister, Fanny, eight, in a fine, comfortable house on the Thames River. His grandfather, called Squire John Ledyard because he was a justice of the peace, was a wealthy, influential merchant and political leader. Squire Ledyard lived in Hartford, Connecticut, with his second wife and their growing family. (He would one day have a total of fifteen children and nearly eighty grandchildren.)

Being the firstborn son of a firstborn son of a firstborn son meant that young John's present as well as his future would be filled with grand advantages and possibilities. He was certain to inherit his father's business as well as a good share of his grandfather's.

Then one day in late March 1762, word arrived that John's father wasn't coming home again.

Captain Ledyard had been stricken with a fever and died on March 17, 1762, in St. Eustatius. Three weeks later, on April 4, Captain Youngs Ledyard,

John's uncle, died of a fever on Money Mountain. No record remains where they were buried or what became of their ship or their cargo.

The news was stark and tragic not only for John's family but for his cousins' as well. Isaac and Ben had become fatherless, too. To make matters worse for John's family, they lost possession of their Groton home. What happened to the deed remains a mystery. Captain Ledyard may have borrowed money against the value of his property, money he could never pay back after the loss of too many ships, too much cargo. Whatever the reason, Abigail was forced to pack up her four children and cross Long Island Sound to live with her family in Southold, New York.

John lost his father, familiar surroundings, and the companionship of his cousins. He once said of his closeness to Isaac and Ben: "We have a language of our own . . . that should Language fail in the communication you would still understand me."

Now he lived among strangers and disapproving Southold relatives. His family's current misfortune stirred up old gossip. There were stories about John's father and mother, first cousins who had eloped to another town to obtain a marriage license. They were forbidden by their families and by law to marry. There were stories about Abigail's missing dowry and her greedy father-in-law's quick-fingered access to property that was hers after Captain Ledyard's death. For eleven-year-old John, this was the first he heard of what he later called "the sins of the family."

Three years after his father's death, John's mother married Dr. Micah Moore, a widower with children of his own. The Southold house was crowded with Dr. Moore's children and John's brothers and sister. In the next five years, three more half sisters would be born, straining the struggling doctor's meager finances.

In 1765, the same year his mother remarried, John's grandfather Squire Ledyard invited John to live with him and his second wife in their prosperous home in Hartford. Here, Squire Ledyard said, he could finish his education. The offer was made even more attractive by including Isaac and Ben in the invitation.

According to one family account, Squire Ledyard extended the offer out of heartbreak over the deaths of his two sons, John's father and uncle—"to replace the sons I lost," he reportedly said. This is possible, although his own home was bursting at the seams with children, including a son named Austin who was exactly John's age.

Times were hard in Connecticut in 1765. The eve of the American Revolution, it was a time of soaring taxes and plummeting land values. People lost their land and were forced into debtors' prison. The colonists blamed the English Stamp Act, which forced them to pay taxes on documents and paper. "A strange Scene of bankruptcy and ruins, the valuable landed interest of the Colony is sunk in its value by more than fifty percent," Squire Ledyard complained in a letter to a friend. Riots broke out. Mobs burned stamp-tax collectors in effigy. They shouted anti-British protests. Radicals talked openly of revolution.

To everyone's relief, the Stamp Act was repealed in 1766. Squire Ledyard, who had been elected deputy of the Colonial Assembly, decided a real celebration was in order. A day of fireworks, bell ringing, speeches, and picnics was planned in Hartford for May 23, 1766. Twenty-one cannons boomed at noon. Amidst the celebrating, drinking, and carousing, a group of young men gathered at the brick schoolhouse to get the fireworks ready for the night's festivities. They may not have realized that the building stored a recent shipment of gunpowder for the militia.

Just twenty yards away, a group of unsuspecting boys discovered a fascinating trail of gunpowder left from the recent delivery. The boys set the sprinkled gunpowder on fire. The stream of powder snapped and crackled, snaking its way through the grass toward the schoolhouse. The air filled with a terrible blast. "In an instant," the *Connecticut Courant* reported, the explosion "reduc'd the Buildings to a heap of Rubbish."

People from Hartford rushed to the accident. It took hours to extricate the bodies of the dead and wounded, among them one of John Ledyard's uncles. Dr. Nathaniel Ledyard's injuries were so severe, he died a week later.

A total of six young men perished. Twenty-four others were injured. Among those injured, though not mentioned in the *Connecticut Courant*, was Austin Ledyard, Squire Ledyard's son who was John Ledyard's age. His

THE   NUMBER 74.

CONNECTICUT COURANT

MONDAY, MAY 26, 1766

HARTFORD,   May 26.

Last Monday Evening the long expected joyful News of the total Repeal of the Stamp Act, arrived in Town : Upon which happy Event, the General Affembly of this Colony, now fetting here, appointed the Friday following, as a Day of general Rejoicing.—The Morning was ufher'd in by the ringing of Bells—the Shipping in the River difplay'd their Colours—at 12 o'Clock 21 Cannon were difcharg'd, and the greateft Preparations making for a general Illumination. Joy fmil'd in every Face ; and univerfal Gladnefs diffus'd itfelf thro' all Ranks and Degrees.—But fudden was the Tranfition from the Height of Joy, to extreme Sorrow! A Number of young Gentlemen were preparing Fire-works for the Evening, in the Chamber of the large Brick-School Houfe ; under which a Quantity of Powder granted by the Affembly for the Purpofes of the Day, was depofited.—Two Companies of Militia had juft received a Pound a Man, by the Delivery of which a Train was fcatter'd from the Pow-der-Cafk to the Diftance of three Rods from the Houfe, where a Number of Boys were collected, who undefignedly and unnotic'd fet Fire to the fcatter'd Powder, which was foon communicated to that within Doors, and in an Inftant reduc'd the Building to a Heap of Rubbifh, and buried the following Perfons in its Ruins, viz.

Mr. Levi Jones, John Knowles [an Apprentice to Mr. Thomas Sloan, Blackfmith] and Richard Lord, fecond Son to Mr. John-Hans Lord,] died of their Wounds, foon afte they were taken from under the Ruins of the Building.

Mr. William Gardiner, Merchant, had both his Legs broke.

Doct. Nathaniel Ledyard, had one of his Thighs broke.

Mr. Samuel Talcott, jun. very much burnt in his Face & Arms.

Mr. James Tiley, Goldfmith, had one of his Sholders diflocated, and fome Bruifes in the other Parts of his Body.

Mr. John Cook, junr. had his Back and Neck much hurt.

Ephraim Perry, flightily wounded.

Thomas Forbes, wounded in his Head.

Daniel Butler, [the Tavern-Keeper's Son] had one of his Ancles put out of Joint.

Richard Burnham, Son to Mr. Elifha Burnham, had his Thigh, Leg, and Ancle broke.

Eli Wadfworth, [Capt. Samuel's Son] is much wounded & burnt, in his Face, Hands, & others Parts of his Body.

John Bunce, junr. [an Apprentice to Mr. Church, Hatter] wounded in the Head.

Normond Morrifon, [a Lad that lives with Capt. Tiley] a good deal burnt and bruifed.

Roderick Lawrence, [Capt. Lawrence's Son] flightily wounded.

William Skinner [Capt. Daniel's Son] had both his Thighs broke.

Timothy Phelps [Son to Mr. Timothy Phelps, Shop-Joiner] had the Calf tore off one of his Legs.

Valentine Vaughn, [Son of Mr. Vaughn, Baker] had his Skull, terribly broke.

Horace Seymour, [Mr. Jonathan Seymour, junr. Son] two Sons of Mr. John Goodwin, a Son of Mr. John Watf on, and a Son of Mr. Kellogg, Hatter, were flightily wounded.

Two Molatto and two Negro Boys, were alfo wounded.

We hear from Suffield, that laft Monday Afternoon, three young Men, were inftantly ftruck dead by a Flafh of Lightning, as they were fitting near a Chimney.

untimely death in 1776 as a young man of twenty-five would later be blamed on the accident.

Who the boys were who caused the explosion may never be known for certain. The tragedy rocked the town for years. Young men grew old bearing scars from the fiery accident. Some were maimed so badly, they were disabled for the rest of their lives. Gossip and blame abounded.

Squire Ledyard did not run again for deputy. He withdrew from public life. What effect the accident had on Squire Ledyard's relationship with his grandson John Ledyard can only be guessed. It is clear, however, that any affection between them began steadily to deteriorate after this point.

In 1771, seventy-one-year-old Squire Ledyard died. On his tombstone was carved: "The memory of the just is blessed." One of his final acts before he died, however, may have seemed less than just to John Ledyard, his namesake. Squire Ledyard left his grandson only sixty pounds in his will—less than half of what he bequeathed to John's cousins Ben and Isaac. To Austin, Squire Ledyard gave all his land and half of his livestock and farming equipment. Despite being the firstborn son of a firstborn son, John Ledyard was essentially cut out of his grandfather's will.

With the death of his grandfather, John was placed under the guardianship of his uncle Thomas Seymour and went to live in his house on Front Street. John finished his schooling in Hartford. Like most men of learning and leisure destined for college, he learned to read Latin and Greek. While his cousin Isaac seemed to be headed for a career in medicine and Ben in business, John still did not have any idea what to do with himself.

Such ordinary considerations never concerned him much. He was not a practical young man. His worst fear was to wake up one morning and discover his life was as dull and ordinary as that of his relatives, who worked hard and never left Connecticut or New York.

"John, be a lawyer," urged his uncle. Thomas Seymour, the vigorous and respectable attorney, woke up every morning and plunged his head and arms into Little River—ice or no. Ledyard tried pleasing his uncle by studying law. He even tried plunging into the river. But law was too boring and the water was too cold.

"John, be a missionary to the heathen Indians," urged John's mother. In 1772, twenty-one-year-old John used what was available from his inheritance and went to study for the ministry at Dartmouth College in Hanover, New Hampshire. Tuition and board was twenty pounds a year. He would have to live very frugally to make his money last.

Being careful with money was not in Ledyard's nature. He tried to liven up the cheerless, newly founded campus in the woods by organizing winter camping trips. (His fellow students complained about the cold.) He attempted to create a theatrical production of *Cato*, a popular play, complete with calico stage curtains and costumes. (His fellow students jeered at his fake long gray beard.)

"His manners were singular," a classmate later wrote. So was his clothing. Always particular about what he wore, he once ordered special Turkish breeches of his own design. He instructed the bewildered tailor in Connecticut to sew the trousers both "loose and snug withal." In an age when most proper upper-class college men wore cravats or ties on formal occasions, Ledyard insisted on keeping his shirt open at the throat. He refused to wear a proper hat.

Finally he could stand the suffocating, drab atmosphere of Dartmouth no longer. Beginning in August 1772, Ledyard disappeared from campus for four months. He claimed he had asked permission. When he returned in December, he said he had gone to Canada to live with the Iroquois. The idea had been for him to convert the Indians to Christianity. Instead, their way of life fascinated him. The Iroquois and their philosophy of life left a lasting impression on Ledyard—not at all what Dartmouth's religious founder, Dr. Eleazar Wheelock, had intended.

When spring returned in 1773, Ledyard became more restless than ever. One balmy day in late April, as the crocuses were poking up through melting snow, Ledyard and a few friends cut down a tree and hollowed out a fifty-foot canoe. Just as Ledyard was no scholar, he was also no woodsman. He injured his foot with the ax.

At last the canoe and its bandaged oarsman were ready. Ledyard packed his pipe, some tobacco, two favorite books of Greek verse, dried venison, and a large bearskin rug. As usual, his exit was dramatic. When Dr. Wheelock was out of sight, Ledyard waved good-bye to his shocked classmates. He climbed into his crude craft and headed 140 miles south to Hartford. He had no map and no real knowledge of the swollen, rushing Connecticut River.

Was Ledyard worried? Absolutely not. He took a nap and let the current carry him along. A few days later, and forty miles downriver, he was so busy

The Reverend Eleazar Wheelock (1711–1779),
who founded Dartmouth College.
Miniature painted by Joseph Steward in 1793.

reading, he almost plunged headlong over thundering Bellows Falls. Just in time he paddled to shore and avoided disaster.

A week or so later, on a bright morning, the first day of May, a group of curious Hartford citizens gathered along the Connecticut River to watch a bear paddle into town. The bear's strange canoe bumped against the shore. With perfect dramatic timing, Ledyard jumped to dry land, triumphantly threw off his bearskin, and revealed his true identity. To Ledyard's immense satisfaction, the crowd applauded.

Uncle Seymour was not so amused. His ne'er-do-well nephew had come home—without a college diploma, without a job, and, worse yet, without any prospects. Ledyard still owed Dartmouth money. He had spent every bit of the extra money Seymour had given him for college. Now that Ledyard had disgraced the family, Uncle Seymour wanted to know, what did he plan on doing with the rest of his life?

Ledyard thought about this question. For several months, he tried half-heartedly to study on his own for the ministry. He wandered about the woods outside of Hartford and practiced sermons using a grove of trees as his congregation. This must have been a strange sight to neighbors, who already considered Ledyard very odd.

That May, he wrote a rambling, angry letter to Dr. Wheelock, who had informed him he was unfit to be a minister. Ledyard was insulted, he said, by Dr. Wheelock's notion that Dartmouth had intended to "save him from utter ruin." Was it his fault, he demanded, that his pitiful legacy was exhausted?

On the back of the letter, two words in Wheelock's handwriting sealed Ledyard's fate: "saucy enough." Wheelock's opinion made it nearly impossible for Ledyard to continue his schooling for the clergy elsewhere. Ledyard did not follow rules, Wheelock said. He was proud, rude, and extravagant. He did not have the right missionary spirit. In short, no church should ever be advised to hire him as a minister.

Ledyard gave up.

Now what profession should he try? He considered going to sea. Perhaps in this way he could make good on his family's honor. He signed aboard a ship belonging to one of his father's old friends, Captain Deshon. The ship was bound for the Barbary Coast with a load of mules.

On December 1, 1773, he left America and went to sea for the first time. "I allot myself a seven years ramble more," Ledyard confided to Isaac after a rough passage to Gibraltar. He arrived in the Mediterranean sometime after January 15.

Although he was as far away as he'd ever been from the watchful eye of his mother, uncle, and other disapproving relatives, his family continued to haunt him. "It is to you that I will turn," he wrote to Isaac, "and for a while forget the curses of those ills I cannot shun." The burden of his family's judgment weighed heavily upon him.

His first voyage wasn't especially glamorous, exciting, or honorable. The food was bad and the weather was terrible. Ledyard decided he'd had enough and mysteriously vanished as soon as the ship docked at Gibraltar. When his captain went to find him, he discovered that Ledyard had signed up with a British regiment. There was Ledyard in the barracks, already dressed in his new uniform.

Ledyard lamely tried to defend himself by saying "he was partial to the service." His captain was unimpressed and dragged the runaway back to the ship. Ledyard was lucky. Ordinarily, a deserter might face court-martial and a term in prison.

When Ledyard returned to Connecticut on September 1, 1774, he was almost twenty-three years old and still uncertain about what he wanted to do with his life. His family was growing impatient. When was he going to settle down and get a job? Ledyard didn't have an answer. Instead, he borrowed more money from his relatives and friends in early 1775 and sailed to England, where he spent many months unsuccessfully rambling around looking for long-lost rich relations he had once heard about from his grandfather. His hope was that they would claim him as one of their own.

While strolling past the docks in London in late spring 1776, Ledyard heard exciting news. Captain Cook was going to sea again.

Immediately, Ledyard made up his mind to enlist. But first he would shave and wash and put on a bright red coat that had once belonged to his grandfather. He must have made something of an impression. Perhaps to his own surprise, Ledyard received a Royal Navy commission as corporal in the marines aboard the flagship *Resolution*—in spite of the fact that he had only been to sea once before and knew practically nothing about guns or military training.

Ah, well, these were details. Practical details that did not matter much to Corporal Ledyard as he began what he hoped would be his life's greatest adventure. If only Uncle Seymour could have seen him now!

Chapter 3

NEW WONDERS

From the Equator to Kerguelen Island
September–December 1776

During the month of September 1776, each passing mile at sea revealed new wonders for Ledyard. Some nights the ocean lit up like liquid fire, the luminous glow of thousands of strange marine creatures. Flying fish as agile as birds skimmed over sun-dappled waves. And always in every direction stretched the startling vastness of sea and sky.

If there seemed too much space outside the ship, on board there was far too little. The 110-foot-long *Resolution*, a little bigger than three modern city buses end to end, had a width of just thirty feet—the length of about one bus. Crammed aboard were enough supplies—food and fresh water—to keep 112 men and numerous cattle alive when no land was in sight, sometimes a month or more at a time.

The 461-ton *Resolution* and the 229-ton *Discovery* were "squat-built" colliers. These stubby vessels were originally used to haul coal. They were the same kind of ships Cook had trained on in the North Sea as a young sailor. During two previous voyages around the world, he had made use of colliers. In fact, the *Resolution* had been the flagship under his last command.

Cook intended for the *Resolution* and the *Discovery* to travel together to aid each other in case of emergency. They were not warships. They were neither large nor fast, compared to other ships that were making round-the-world voyages at the time. There was nothing fancy, streamlined, or impressive-looking about the square-rigged vessels. Neither even had the simplest figurehead carving of a mermaid or a smiling woman at the bow, or front. Cook preferred colliers because they were sturdy. They could travel in fairly shallow water and could be brought ashore, overturned, and repaired if necessary. And they could carry lots of supplies.

Stowed below on the *Resolution* were forty bushels of white bay salt; thirty quarts of best wheat; 580 pounds of beef to be salted; 1,800 gallons of spirits, wine, and beer; and 3,400 pounds of the best, dark muscovado sugar—raw sugar created after molasses was extracted from sugarcane. Also stored aboard was a six-month supply of "ship biscuit," or hard crackers, barrels of dried peas, and vinegar and oil. Antiscorbutics, or scurvy-preventing foods, included half a ton of "portable soup," brown slabs of gluey meat extract to be boiled with oatmeal; and a year's supply of sauerkraut, or pickled cabbage, a German dish—enough for each man to have two pounds a week. There were eighty bushels of malt, dried yeast, and pressed hops in storage for use in making healthful spruce beer. Added to all this was a six-month supply of fresh water, crates of cheese and butter, and experimentally packed bread.

Since the expedition would be traveling in arctic cold as well as warm South Sea climates, each man had to have a pair of heavy trousers, thick woolen "fearnought" jackets, and "four or five good Watch coats." The *Resolution* contained 800 pairs of shoes, 340 red woolen caps, and 440 shirts.

Coal and timber for fuel and eight tons of ballast took up enormous amounts of space. Ship's ballast was usually sandbags or gravel stored in the vessel's lower area to keep the heavy mast and rigging above deck from tipping over the ship.

For protection, the *Resolution* was armed with twelve four-pounders, or small cannons; twelve swivel guns; and twelve musketoons, or short, stout muskets. Fifty barrels of musket powder were stored in the magazine, an enclosed space above deck guarded by marines, who were supposed to make sure no one entered with a lighted lantern and blew the ship to pieces.

The *Resolution* carried twenty cork jackets (life jackets), stationery, a distilling machine for "sweetening foul water," a special lifesaving device for a man overboard—a wooden pole with a bell on one end and cork supports—and "an apparatus for recovering drowned persons" (in case the lifesaving device did not work).

To trade with natives for fresh food and vegetables, the *Resolution* had to have plenty of "trifles and trinkets": two hundred axes, half a ton of nails, twenty-four dozen knives, and twenty dozen fishhooks—all made from iron. Popular with natives were files, saws, scissors, mirrors, beads, bundles of bright red feathers (a Tahitian favorite), and baby dolls. Special gifts, such as tricornered hats, silk dressing gowns, and English top hats, were always welcomed by high-ranking chiefs and other native dignitaries.

Living and working space aboard the *Resolution* was reduced even further by the barnyard of noisy, hungry animals penned on deck. Donated by King George (nicknamed "Farmer George"), the animals were to be given by Cook to South Sea natives to encourage "civilized" English-style farming. In addition to one bull, two cows with calves, a large number of sheep and rabbits, one mare, a stallion, assorted pigs, and a peacock and hen, the king insisted that Cook also distribute barrels of grass, mustard, and barley seed.

Other *Resolution* livestock included several goats for officers' milk, hens and a rooster for officers' fresh eggs and meat, and a menagerie of pets—dogs and cats—that wandered freely above and below deck. "Thus did we resemble an ark," Ledyard wrote, "and appear as though we were going as well to stock, as to discover a new world."

The *Resolution* was first and foremost a vessel of discovery, a roaming scientific research station with the most sophisticated technology available. Cook always insisted on the very latest advances in navigational equipment. Room had to be made for sensitive compasses, telescopes, sextants, barometers, thermometers, and chronometers. These temperamental devices had to be guarded from curious natives and kept in good working order—even in rough seas. Scientists on board brought all kinds of equipment: a library of reference books, machines for catching and preserving insects, nets, trawls, hooks for coral fishing, an underwater telescope, and cases of fragile bottles with stoppers to preserve animals in spirits.

For Ledyard and the other men on board, the first exciting land sighting came on October 1, 1776, when a lookout spied the Cape of Good Hope, the southernmost tip of Africa. Colonized by the Dutch, this port was the last European jumping-off place they visited before they entered the Pacific.

The *Resolution* anchored at Table Bay. To Ledyard the surrounding landscape seemed rocky and mountainous, "very romantic and somehow majestically great by nature." Others weren't so impressed and called the Dutch settlement "the barrenest spot upon earth."

Perhaps Ledyard was swept away with enthusiasm because this was his first chance to go ashore in his fancy uniform: white knee-length breeches and a high-collared red jacket with silk-fringe epaulets and shiny gilt buttons. He marched off the ship in his cocked hat and his boots with tall black gaiters and buttons on the side—all of which had been kept neat and orderly in his sea chest stowed away below deck.

Ledyard and the other marines were ordered to set up and guard the astronomical instruments on shore and establish an observatory for Second Lieutenant James King. The fussy twenty-six-year-old son of a Lancashire minister was supposed to assist the astronomer. Tents were also set up for sail makers, coopers, and carpenters, who went to work making repairs on the ship. Cattle and sheep were brought on shore to graze in hastily constructed pens.

Still there was no sight of the *Discovery*.

Supplies of food, fodder, and fresh water were loaded onto the ship. Cook sent special orders for the bakers in town to begin making ship biscuit, the hard crackers that would last for many months at sea. Unfortunately, the work began later than Cook anticipated and he was very impatient with the Dutch suppliers, whom he accused of attempting to "get as much by strangers as they possibly can." When almost the entire herd of sheep mysteriously disappeared one night, Cook was outraged.

Unlike Cook, Ledyard was delighted by the place. To him it appeared an admirable settlement of thirty tidy houses, surrounded by vineyards and

This set of navigational instruments was among the many devices Cook took on his voyage. The wooden box contains (from top to bottom) a table of star signs and dates, compass, spirit level sundial, astrolabe, and measuring instrument.

orchards. He was impressed by the Dutch, whose industry had made the barren land productive. He was especially pleased by the wine.

Among the *Resolution* travelers was a dark-skinned Tahitian in his mid-twenties named Omai. It's hard to imagine what the suspicious Dutch Cape Town inhabitants thought of him as he strutted up and down their streets in his velvet English suit and inspected with curiosity and disdain the few items they had for sale. Omai was not impressed with Cape Town. Nothing could compare with the past two years of material pleasures and experiences with which he had been showered back in London.

Omai was a celebrity who was making the journey on the *Resolution* in order to return to his homeland in the South Pacific. He had been brought to England in 1774 as part of the exotic cultural "curiosities" of Cook's second voyage to Otaheite, or Tahiti. When Omai arrived, London newspapers called him "the wild Indian, that was taken on an island in the South Seas."

The cheerful, tattooed native became an overnight London sensation. When introduced to King George, Omai was said to have exclaimed, "How do, King Tosh!" Though his English was far from perfect (he called Captain Cook "Toot"), Omai made every effort to please and imitate his English hosts. London intellectuals and members of high society made Omai into something of a pet. The popular philosophy of the time extolled the virtues of "noble savages," superior beings who lived in close harmony with nature.

The king had wisely insisted that Omai be inoculated against smallpox—an act that may have saved his life. King George generously gave Omai an allowance and set him up in his own house on Warwick Street. He was presented by the king with a fancy sword and a suit of armor. Omai learned how to bow, flourish his sword, play cards, and shoot game birds (and chickens alike). In a fine velvet suit with lace cuffs he attended the House of Lords, went to church at St. James, attended the opera, learned how to ice-skate, and struggled to learn to ride a horse.

When King George announced that it was time for Omai to go home, Cook was assigned the task of returning him and his numerous souvenirs. The hold of the *Resolution* was crammed with Omai's medieval armor, muskets, English bed, assorted chairs and tables, collection of tin soldiers, hand organ, globe, enormous color Bible, uncounted crates of crockery and kitchenware, kegs of port wine, and a jack-in-the-box complete with toy snake to scare and impress the natives back home.

Omai had a "great good Nature and docile disposition," Cook later wrote. "He had a tolerable share of understanding. He was not a man of much observation." Ledyard and many of the other sailors spoke more frankly about Omai, whom they found dim-witted, bossy, and ridiculous. Ledyard was among the many seamen who grumbled loudly at Table Bay when Cook added even more cattle—all to be taken to Tahiti for Omai. Crowded into their already cramped living arrangement were four horses, three young bulls, three heifers, twenty goats, and a good number of sheep.

When the *Discovery* was sighted on November 10 coming into the bay, the crew of the *Resolution* cheered. Ledyard and the rest of the marines fired off thirteen guns in greeting. When the *Discovery* came closer, disturbing news arrived for Ledyard. The corporal of marines on the *Discovery* had drowned en route.

Corporal George Harrison of the *Discovery*, who held the same job as Led-

In 1774 Sir Joshua Reynolds sketched the exotic London visitor Omai in pencil.

yard, had fallen overboard while sitting carelessly on the bowsprit. The only thing the *Discovery* sailors managed to retrieve from the water was his Dutch cap. Sharks, they said, got the rest.

There was little time to reflect on Harrison's death. All hands were needed to trim the sails and haul aboard the last supplies. Hurried letters were mailed home. This might be the last opportunity to send word back to Europe for three, maybe four years.

Cook passed his secret instructions to Clerke, who had been ordered not to open them without authority unless the ships were separated. Finally, on November 23, 1776, the *Resolution* and the *Discovery* left Table Bay. "We took our departure from this great promontory," Ledyard wrote, "and launched into that immense ocean which surrounds so great a part of the southern hemisphere."

Shipboard rumors flew. Were they simply returning Omai to Tahiti? Or was the expedition actually in search of new Pacific islands to claim for the British crown? No one aboard the *Resolution* or *Discovery* knew where the expedition was ultimately headed.

Orders from the Admiralty were sealed in wax inside a parchment envelope and kept under lock and key. Only Cook knew for certain of the ships' destination and prize: the Northwest Passage.

For nearly two centuries, the Northwest Passage had conjured up dreams of wealth and riches for European monarchs, merchants, and sailors alike. The Northwest Passage was believed to be an ice-free seaway through the northern reaches of North America connecting the Pacific and the Atlantic—a shortcut for trade between Europe and the marvelous spice islands of the Orient.

The Admiralty's top secret instructions for the *Resolution* and the *Discovery* were to sail around the Cape of Good Hope, restock food supplies in Tahiti, deposit Omai and all his many new European belongings, and hurry directly to North America's largely uncharted western coast, near present-day Monterey, California. The ships were then to head north to what is now Sealawik, Alaska. At this point, the expedition was "very carefully to search for and to explore, such Rivers or Inlets as may appear to be of a considerable extent, and pointing toward Hudsons or Baffin Bay."

If the Pacific entrance to the Northwest Passage were found, Cook was to sail east to the Atlantic. The Admiralty believed that the passage would somehow empty either into Baffin or Hudson Bay, in what is now central Canada. There, Cook's expedition would be met by the *Lyon*, under the command of British Captain Richard Pickersgill.

If all went as planned, the *Resolution*, the *Discovery*, and the *Lyon* were to sail home to England in 1777 or at the latest 1778. And what a triumphant return they would have! Commanders and crew could expect to become not only famous but rich, too. Since 1745, British Parliament had offered the fabulous sum of twenty thousand pounds (roughly half a million dollars in current American currency) to the first expedition to locate and sail successfully through the Northwest Passage. As yet, no one had been able to claim the reward.

More than fifty European explorers had tried to find an entrance to the passage from the Atlantic. All had failed. Captain Cook was attacking the problem in a bold new way. His Pacific route was being kept secret in hopes of preventing England's competitors, France and Spain, from copying or thwarting the plan.

When information about the true destination eventually leaked among European courts, Captain Cook's expedition was already far away. After the American ambassador to France, Benjamin Franklin, heard about the voyage, he was so sure of Cook's triumphant discovery of the Northwest Passage—and eager for America to benefit—that he wrote an order prohibiting American armed ships at war with England from attacking either the *Resolution* or the *Discovery*. "Treat Captain Cook and his people with all civility and kindness," Franklin warned.

While the heads of state back home discussed the expedition, neither ship's crew knew its destination. Hale and hearty now after nearly four weeks on rations of fresh meat and vegetables, Ledyard and the other sailors left Africa filled with high hopes.

Upon entering the southern Indian Ocean, they immediately hit bad storms and "a constant series of fogs," according to Ledyard. Temperatures plunged. Ledyard and the crew hastily exchanged their thin jackets for wool-lined fearnought jackets with hoods.

The seas swelled from the west. On December 5, high winds ripped off the mizzen topmast. Waves crashed over the deck. Water rushed down the hatches. Ledyard and the others sloshed below deck in icy, ankle-deep water. It was, Clerke wrote on December 16, "24 hours of nasty, raw, wet, disagreeable Weather."

Livestock shrieked and skidded across the wet deck. Terrified horses bucked. The men's tempers flared. In the midst of the storm, two *Resolution* marines got into a fight that would cost them six lashes each in punishment.

The foggy weather kept an iron grip on the ships. Guns were fired every hour so the ships could try to keep track of each other. The *Resolution* and *Discovery* tried to stay together as much as safety would allow. Already the season was slipping away. There was no time to lose.

On Christmas Eve they spied through the fog a rocky, mountainous island dusted with snow. Kerguelen Island (also called Desolation Island) was 3,300 miles southeast of the Cape of Good Hope. This would be the last dismal fragment of land until the continent now called Australia.

Ledyard and several of the other officers pulled out notebooks to record their impressions. John Webber, the official expedition artist from Germany who was a year younger than Ledyard, made quick sketches.

A promising-looking bay was discovered and the marines were sent ashore in smaller boats to check to make sure the water was deep enough for the *Resolution* and *Discovery*. Cook sent some marines with water casks to shore to collect fresh water, which was found in gullies. Unfortunately, not much was discovered in the way of fuel. "Not a single tree or shrub," Cook wrote.

There were plenty of seals and birds, including penguins so unfamiliar with people that they made easy targets for sailors with clubs. For some of the crew, the penguins' melancholy croaking on the foggy, raw, cold island was unnerving. Marines and several sailors were sent ashore to cut grass for the livestock and kill seals for oil.

Ledyard was delighted to be rambling on shore when a discovery was made. "A glass bottle suspended by a wire between two rocks: it was corked and sealed over with a parchment within it," he wrote. The bottle was brought to Captain Cook. The message, written in Latin, indicated that the French

The sandy shores of Christmas Harbor in Kerguelen's Land (now known as Kerguelen Island) abounded with docile penguins easily clubbed by sailors for meat and lamp oil.

had already visited the island in 1772 and 1773 and claimed it for King Louis the Fifteenth.

Cook scribbled in his own comments, announcing the arrival of his two ships and claiming the land for Britain in the year 1776. The crew built a pile of rocks over the lead-capped bottle and raised the Union Jack flag of England. This seemed to cheer most of the men, although ship's surgeon William Anderson thought the ceremony ridiculous. What was the point of taking possession of an island populated mostly by penguins? Nothing else about the place was the least bit delightful. Ledyard described it as "ragged, detached, and almost totally barren."

Ledyard and other marines combed the shore for whatever greenery they could find. No one knew when they'd be on land again. Plant-gathering expeditions were a regular duty on Cook's voyages. Green plants were cooked and fed to the crews, who were often reluctant to try anything new. The reason for the culinary experiments was to prevent scurvy, a killer on long-distance voyages. This dreaded disease, known as "the great enemy" among sailors, wiped out more crews than drowning and gunfire combined. Scurvy's symptoms began as aching muscles, tender gums, and loose teeth. Soon, sailors complained of being tired. They became too weak to handle duties aboard ship. In the final stages of the disease, uncontrollable bleeding and eventual starvation occurred.

Scurvy occurred when fresh vegetables and fruits containing vitamin C were not available over extended periods of time. There was simply no way to refrigerate and store fruits and vegetables aboard ship. Cook brought along the latest in prepackaged foods, hoping this would prevent scurvy: portable soup; sauerkraut; powdered malt, known as wort; and barrels of boiled citrus syrup that had been preserved in sugar.

Cook was no scientist, but he knew from practical experience that if he fed his crew vegetables, they did not come down with scurvy. He was an avid experimenter. On Kerguelen, the wild cabbage Ledyard and the other men gathered up was "as wretched as the soil it was indigenous to," Ledyard wrote. The cabbage wasn't bad raw but when boiled, Anderson said, "it seemed to acquire a rank flavour."

There was no special dinner on Christmas Day. Cook did not pause in charting the island's coast and sounding the depths of the water. There were no religious services, no extra grog. Some of the men grumbled. "Never before had experienced Christmas day so little noticed," wrote an anonymous sailor.

On December 27, Cook relented and gave his crew the day off "to celibrate Christmas." Double rations of grog were served to "each common man." Wine and spirits were distributed among petty officers.

When the *Resolution* and *Discovery* finally set sail on December 29, no one was sad to leave. "Perhaps," wrote Cook, "no place hitherto discovered in either Hemisphere under the same parallel of latitude afford[s] so scanty a field for the naturalist as this barren spot." Immediately, two young bulls, a heifer, most of the goats and two rams died—perhaps from eating grass brought on board that had been fouled by penguin dung.

Although Ledyard and the others may have been secretly pleased to see the number of bothersome stock on board dwindle, the situation gave Cook cause for concern. He had been strictly instructed by the Crown to take as many animals as possible into the "new world" to convince the savages to take up farming and cattle raising and abandon "cannibal habits."

Little did Ledyard or anyone else realize what effect the responsibility of this cargo would have on the voyage—and on their captain.

Chapter 4

EXOTIC ANCHORAGES

From Kerguelen Island to New Zealand
December 1776–February 1777

To picture traveling the Pacific in the eighteenth century is to imagine a journey into the far reaches of outer space. Sailors, like Ledyard and the others aboard the *Resolution* and *Discovery,* might be gone from home for years. Wooden sailing ships—the most sophisticated pieces of technology created at the time—crossed boundless stretches of water on round-the-world voyages. Deepwater sailors might not see land for weeks or months.

What made these journeys so difficult and dangerous was that fresh food and water could be resupplied for such large crews only on land. And the only refueling stops in the Pacific (if they could be successfully located) were small, often hostile islands called coral atolls. These horseshoe-shaped islands were surrounded by high surf that beat against fortresslike underwater walls of razor-sharp coral.

If a ship was lucky enough to send a crew ashore successfully in a smaller boat, the landing party might not find fresh water or anything edible. Sometimes the best they could discover would be a few coconuts, a kind of banana called a plantain, and scrawny seabirds. Often more bountiful islands were populated by unfriendly native people, who almost always outnumbered the crew. It would be simply too dangerous to go ashore to take advantage of the resources.

The original directions given by the Admiralty had ordered Cook to sail from the Cape of Good Hope in Africa to Tahiti, a total of nearly eleven thousand miles. Their only stop was to be a brief layover in New Zealand, if necessary. Now it was early January 1777. They were already nearly two months behind schedule and the weather was not cooperating. For the next two weeks, Ledyard and the rest of the crews aboard the *Resolution* and *Discovery* were tossed by high seas. "Hard gales of wind . . . lost one of our topmasts, and were other wise very roughly dealt with," Ledyard wrote.

Water funneled through open seams in the sides of the hull. Temporary caulking had not done the job. During a lull in the bad weather, the *Resolution*'s carpenters struggled to repair gaps. The main topgallant had to be repaired as well, since there was no spare. More time was lost.

When they were able to resume their journey, the fog became too thick to see more than a "quarter mile ahead." The ships signaled to each other to keep track of their whereabouts. Men shouted back and forth. No one was certain what lay ahead—island, rock, or shoal.

On January 24 the weather miraculously cleared. A lookout spotted the southernmost tip of the island of Van Diemen's Land, now called Tasmania, located southeast of Australia. The weather was mild. Sheltered here was a place Cook had named Adventure Bay on an earlier voyage. Ledyard and the others saw it as a welcome place—a white sand beach, plenty of trees, and fresh water flowing in small streams. The only ominous signs were puffs of smoke from native campfires rising from the interior of the island.

As soon as the ships moored on January 26, Ledyard and the other marines were sent ashore in a pinnace, a boat with oars. Work parties were sent ashore to cut wood, gather grass, and collect water in barrels. William Bayly, the expedition's astronomer, set up his tent to make observations. Carpenters went to work. While rigging was repaired, nets were cast to catch fish. With the marines serving as guards, officers and gentlemen went on shore to "take a view of this delightful country," said *Discovery* Second Lieutenant John Rickman, "with the appear[a]nce of which all on board were charmed."

The marines from the *Discovery* took advantage of the lovely weather and relative freedom to steal bottles of liquor. They began drinking, forgot their

A man of Van Diemen's Land (now known as Tasmania) greeted Ledyard and the crew without weapon, ornament, or clothing.

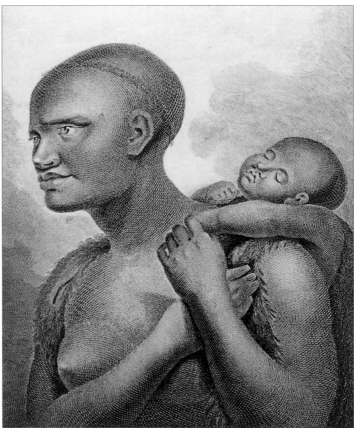

A woman of Van Diemen's Land tenderly carried her sleeping baby on her back.

jobs completely, and were soon dead drunk on the beach. They were dragged back to the ship, hauled aboard unconscious, and later punished with a dozen lashes, double the usual punishment. The marines, who were supposed to be the crew's only defense against surprise attack, clearly did not take their jobs seriously.

After the boats had been moored in the harbor for three days, nine curious natives appeared between the trees where the marines and others were cutting firewood. The short, dark natives were completely naked and did not seem surprised by the first white men they had probably ever encountered. They crept closer, fascinated by the sailors' clothing, which they may have assumed was part of their strange visitors' bodies.

They examined the water casks with curiosity. The boats seemed to amaze them. One of them got hold of a rope and began to haul it to shore for a closer look. The officer made signs for them to stop. They refused. The officer shot his gun into the air, terrifying the visitors so badly that they ran into the woods.

The natives' eyes, William Anderson said, were what connected him to the familiar and gave "a frank, cheerful cast to the whole countenance." Anderson found these natives neither fierce nor wild. He described them as "mild and cheerfull without reserve or jealousy of strangers"—something he only noticed among natives who had never encountered Europeans before. "Their features were far from disagreeable," wrote Cook, who wasn't especially descriptive. "They had pretty good eyes and their teeth were tolerable even but very dirty."

The only weapons the natives carried were sharp sticks, presumed to be used for hunting. The men's skin was decorated with scars that may have been incised with a knife to denote initiation into manhood.

This was Ledyard's first chance to observe natives in their own environment. He described them as "of a dark complexion bordering on black, their hair a little wooly." He found them "ignoble inhabitants" living in paradise. Always conscious of dress, Ledyard was perplexed by their nakedness and described "their features discordant and without any kind of ornament." He could not understand why people living in an abundant forest had no weapons. Why were their houses only pieces of bark laid across poles? Why did people with access to the sea have no canoes and no fishhooks?

Ledyard came up with his own theory: "They appear to be inactive, indolent and unaffected with the least appearance of curiosity." Since no one knew the native people's language, little could be learned about them.

Using crude sign language, an officer offered a native man fish to eat. The native was horrified and refused. Fish was forbidden, Cook's men assumed. A pile of shells seemed to indicate that shellfish was the only food they ate.

The women would have nothing to do with the sailors, even though they were bribed with special gifts. Like the men, they set no value in iron tools.

Omai, always the show-off, decided to impress the natives by shooting a musket. The noise terrified them and they fled into the forest, leaving behind their gifts of an ax and two knives. Later, when they felt safe enough to return, Cook presented them with some beads, some red cloth, and "other trinkets." When one of the natives touched Cook's jacket, Cook gave that to him as well. Cook left a boar and a sow in the woods, hoping that they would survive and eventually furnish food for the "primitives."

There was both a remarkable tolerance and intolerance toward the people of Tasmania. They had not been exposed enough to white sailors to fear them or find them worth plundering. This reassured Cook, who preferred natives who "knew their place." On the other hand, Ledyard clearly thought them unworthy of consideration as "interesting" because they didn't create any art or culture that he could discover, given that their language was a mystery.

After three days in Adventure Bay, Cook suddenly announced that they were going to pull up anchor and sail to New Zealand. The men quickly disassembled the tents, brought them on board, and weighed anchor. New Zealand wasn't in the official itinerary. It had been described in the Admiralty's directions as a stopover only if Cook saw fit. The detour would cost them time.

On February 1, 1777, the ships left Adventure Bay. In the next twelve days, they encountered heavy seas and rain. Ledyard must have been alarmed to hear of another drowned marine. George Moody, a private aboard the

The inside of a hippah, *or fortress, in New Zealand*

Discovery, who had been one of the four drunks found on the beach at Adventure Bay, fell overboard February 5—presumably drunk again. Cook made a short note in his log: "This was the second Marine Captain Clerke had had the Missfortune to lose sence he left England."

This seemed a bad sign to the many sailors and officers who had sailed with Cook on the second voyage to Ship Cove, New Zealand. It had been here in December 1774 that First Lieutenant James "Jem" Burney, now aboard the *Discovery,* discovered that a missing crew of grass cutters had been attacked and eaten by Maori cannibals. "Such a shocking scene of carnage and barbarity," wrote Burney, "as can never be mentioned or thought of but with horror."

Omai, aboard the *Resolution,* had also witnessed the carnage. In his traditional way of thinking, the only option was revenge.

As the two ships sailed into Queen Charlotte Sound, Ledyard heard the stories again. For the protection of the crews on shore, Cook ordered ten marines to stand guard and gave each crew member a gun. "A boat was never sent any considerable distance from the ships without being armed, and under the direction of such officers as I could depend upon and who were well acquainted with the Natives."

The atmosphere for Ledyard and the other marines was tense. They nervously scanned the trees for any sign of Maoris after being sent ashore January 12. They were to act as guards for the men shouldering water casks, setting up the astronomy observatory tent, and cutting grass for cattle fodder. A small work party chopped off the green tops of spruce pines and boiled these in kettles. The liquid, mixed with malt, dried yeast, and hops, would be used to make spruce beer, which Cook served on all his expeditions to prevent scurvy.

The *Resolution* had been anchored only a short while before canoes filled with nervous, mistrustful Maoris came alongside the ship. They waved branches to indicate they came in peace. What would Cook do? Had he come back for revenge? What was Omai, the familiar but strange-looking character they remembered from a previous voyage, doing on board? Omai waved a fancy white handkerchief and called to them in their language.

When it was clear that Cook did not intend revenge, entire families showed up on the beach and set up temporary shelters with branches and huts. Soon the smoky smell of cook fires filled the air. There were the sounds of dogs barking, children laughing, and women gossiping.

Having the natives close at hand made some of the veteran sailors fearful. Others who had not sailed with Cook before found that the natives' presence made life easier and, perhaps, a bit more familiar and domestic. The men could trade easily with the natives, who were more than happy to provide excellent-tasting fish in exchange for nails, fishhooks, and red cloth.

Life ashore took on a predictable rhythm. Portable soup was boiled with peas and wheat every day. Celery and scurvy grass, a plant with heart-shaped leaves and tar-like flavor, were served. Cook stopped the issue of grog and instead insisted that the men drink spruce beer. Even this did not seem like much of a hardship.

Ledyard was among the crew members who felt little anxiety about the Maoris or their reputation. He described them as "generally well-made, strong and robust" and was especially impressed with the chiefs. "When a New-Zealander stands forth and brandishes his spear the subsequent idea is . . . there stands a man."

As one of the guards stationed on land, Ledyard had plenty of opportunity to observe the Maoris. Their clothing, he said, looked like a kind of toga, a waterproof woven covering made from grass and dog hair that hung from the shoulders. "They paint their faces with a coarse red paint, and oil or grease the head and upper part of the body." Men and women both wore their hair long in a topknot. "They are curiously tattooed about the face."

Ledyard pointed to "their ferocious manners" as the reason no one had much information about them. He tried to find out where they came from and what their religion was but had little luck except to record that their ancestors long, long ago came from a far distant island called "Hawyjee."

Unlike Ledyard, many of the other sailors were preoccupied by the cannibal rumors of the warlike Maoris. To Anderson, who was usually fairly forgiving, the natives were "of a suspicious or mistrustfull temper."

Many of the sailors found the Maoris unpleasant-smelling and strange-looking. "The savageness of their dispositions and horrid barbarity of their customs is fully expressed in their countenances," wrote eighteen-year-old midshipman George Gilbert, "which is ferocious and frightful beyond immagination."

For once Cook and his men could communicate through a translator. Omai, whose English was certainly not as good as his card playing, spoke a kind of pidgin Maori based on his native tongue, Tahitian. He was the one man from the former expedition that the Maoris recognized. He became the main translator, even though Ledyard's superior, Royal Marine Sergeant Samuel Gibson, a veteran of two voyages with Cook, spoke Tahitian well and could understand Maori. Unfortunately, Omai's enthusiasm for revenge sometimes colored his interpretations.

The encounter soon proved to be an uneasy peace.

Captain Cook decided to find out exactly what had happened to his men on the previous expedition. As soon as he sent five boats and sixty men to Grass Cove, the place where the murders had taken place, the natives became visibly nervous. Cook tried interviewing a family living nearby. Most of what he discovered had to do with a quarrel over bread that escalated into a massacre.

"They told us," Cook said, "that while our people were at victuals with several of the natives about them some of the latter stole or snatched from them some bread, & fish for which they were beat this being resented a quarrel ensued, in which two of the Natives were shot dead, by the only two Muskets that were fired, for before they had time to discharge a third or load those that were fired they were all seized and knocked on the head."

It's not surprising perhaps that the tension almost broke into another massacre situation when Sergeant Gibson got into a shouting match with a Maori chief. Gibson was not a man to back down in a fight. On this particular day he and the other marines were supposed to keep the natives out of the astronomical tent—always a favorite place for thievery. The invaluable, shiny metal telescopes, quadrants, and compasses fascinated the Maoris.

When Gibson warned the Maori chief to keep away, the chief shouted vengeance at Gibson and jumped in his canoe to collect reinforcements. Someone still on board the *Resolution* saw what was happening. Cook ordered that the remaining marines row the pinnace as fast as they could and cut off the growing war party.

Fortunately, that was as far as the violence escalated.

There was an uncertainty about the eleven days in New Zealand that put everyone on edge. "The Seamen had taken a kind of dislike to these people," Cook noted in his journal, "and were unwilling or affraid to associate with them." Cook noted that New Zealanders lived under "perpetual apprehensions of being destroyed by each other." Cannibalism was the ultimate act of Maori revenge.

One day the chief named Kahura, who had supposedly killed men from the crew at Grass Cove, suddenly appeared on board the *Resolution*. Omai did not understand why Cook did not pounce on the chance to murder the chief. In England, he reminded Cook, a murderer would be hanged.

Cook refused to seek vengeance. The next time Kahura came to visit, Cook asked him again why the murders were committed. Kahura only folded his arms in front of himself and refused to answer.

When Kahura was sure Cook wouldn't punish him, the Maori turned cocky. Paint my portrait, he demanded. Webber obliged. Kahura sat very still.

When the portrait was finished, Cook warned Kahura that should he or any of his tribesmen make a second murder attempt, "they might rest assured of feeling the weight of my resentment."

Kahura was not impressed. Revenge was a Maori way of life.

In spite of these incidents with the unpredictable, often violent New Zealanders, Ledyard heard a curious story about a young crew member from the *Discovery* who fell in love with a fourteen-year-old Maori girl and ran away into the hills with her. According to the tale, she had been forbidden to speak of the Grass Cove incident. A "rugged guard" captured the sailor, brought him back, and sat him before Cook—who forgave him.

This extravagant story recalls an episode on Cook's first voyage, when then-Private Samuel Gibson fell in love with a Tahitian woman, had himself tattooed, and tried to desert and run off with her. He was brought back and flogged. Later, his knowledge of Tahitian helped save the life of Cook, who was so impressed with Gibson he took him on two more voyages.

Ledyard, always the romantic, seemed fascinated by the runaway incident in New Zealand. He may have first come across the story in a fanciful article published by the crews of the *Discovery* and *Resolution* in their regular newspaper. Whenever the newspaper was ready for delivery and the weather was fair, a boat went out to exchange copies between ships. Cook was always glad to read the homemade newspaper but never favored the publication with any articles.

When Cook announced that they would soon make ready to sail again, two passengers from New Zealand were taken on board the *Resolution*. Omai insisted on having two young boys as servants on the new farm he was to be given when he arrived back in Tahiti. Nine-year-old Coaa accompanied his master, seventeen-year-old Tiarooa, who was the son of a chief. Cook had tried to make clear to the older boy's mother that they would never be coming back again. It wasn't until the *Resolution* actually set sail that she became "inconsolable with grief."

By then it was too late.

Ledyard wondered about shipboard gossip that said the boys had been secretly purchased. Unfortunately, after the ship was under way, the seasick boys began to howl with grief—a situation that made life for the next seven days very unpleasant for everyone on board. The boys sobbed and sang sad songs for their lost friends and family and country. They wept openly at night when they were alone. Cook tried to cheer them up by ordering red cloth made into jackets for each of them. Even these did not help.

After the first week rolled by, the sadness began to disappear. Eventually the boys became great favorites of Ledyard and the other sailors. Lively Coaa performed the role of jokester. He mimicked the speech and actions of certain crew members, who found the performance very funny. His master, "a sedate sensible young fellow," did not engage in so many antics, but was "universally liked" nonetheless.

Ledyard described Tiarooa as "stout and well made but of a ferocious gloomy aspect." Of the two boys, he was more impressed by Coaa, "a young lively agreeable child." The boys' welcome presence made Ledyard recall pleasant scenes from his own childhood. For homesick fathers among the sailors, the sounds of young voices and laughter had a bittersweet quality. When, they wondered, would they see their own children again?

Chapter 5

"Our Imaginary Greatness"

From New Zealand to Tonga
February–June 1777

Whatever patience Cook managed to display toward the natives of New Zealand he would never show again. He was not by nature a patient man. And whatever reserves of patience he had were being slowly eroded by unseen forces deep in his own gut. Ledyard and the others could see the strain on their captain's face—the taut lines around his mouth, his scowling glare. Cook's temper, never easily controlled, flared with an unpredictability that began to surprise even the veterans of his other voyages.

Cook's ships were supposed to reconnoiter by late summer with the British ship the *Lyon* in central Canada—more than 8,500 miles away. If everything went as planned, they'd barely make the rendezvous in time. But of course, nothing was going as planned.

Delays dogged the expedition. As soon as the *Resolution* and *Discovery* left Queen Charlotte Sound on February 24, 1777, the wind began to play tricks. Throughout the month of March, the ship was forced off course to the north. The journey from New Zealand to Tahiti took weeks instead of days. Limited hay for cattle dwindled. Sheep were killed so that cattle, which were larger and more valued, could live.

The wind died to a calm. Sails sagged. The ship rocked on low swells—not going anywhere. Ledyard and the other idle men waited hopelessly for the westerly trade winds to carry them in a wide curve to the north. From there the southeasterly winds would push them the rest of the way to the Society Islands, where Tahiti was located.

For days nothing happened.

Long voyages, a traveler once wrote, require a bustle every now and then to keep the devil out of the sailors' heads. Without enough to do aboard the *Resolution,* complaints arose. Boredom encouraged thefts of officers' food. Cook was in no mood to deal with such behavior. He cut everyone's meat rations until the culprit could be found. In response, the men refused meat altogether, claiming the punishment unfair. "A very mutinous proceeding," Cook barked, showing none of his usual skill in handling conflicts with his men.

Between the complaints of the men and the pitiful crying of starving cattle, life aboard the *Resolution* was becoming steadily disagreeable.

Finally, on March 29, the watch aboard the *Discovery* spied land in the distance. A special flag was unfurled. The atoll, later named Mangaia, was part of a group of islands previously undiscovered by Europeans. They would later be named the Lower Cooks or Southern Cook Group in honor of Cook. This gave the men hope. Perhaps their captain's luck had returned.

Ledyard and others on board the *Resolution* and *Discovery* looked out at the flat white beach fringed with trees. Encircling the atoll was a deadly ring of surf. There was no way the two large ships could go any closer because of the coral reef's jagged edges. Through the telescope, Ledyard could see natives gathering on the distant beach. They waved spears and shouted threats. An unpromising sign.

Neither Ledyard nor any of the other marines were sent ashore. Not yet.

One small canoe approached. Omai, who was still serving as interpreter, shouted greetings from the *Resolution* and was surprised to discover that he could understand the strangers. He called to them. Some beads and red cloth tied to a piece of wood were tossed overboard. The natives paddled closer and picked up the gift, which they "viewed with great Astonishment," David Samwell, surgeon's first mate, reported. Had they never seen white explorers before?

Ledyard watched as the natives' canoe floated near enough for them to catch a red shirt thrown by Cook. One man, who did not seem terrified, came even closer. "As soon as he was near enough to us," Ledyard said, "we shewed him several European trinkets and made such signs to him, as we thought he would best understand meaning to conciliate his good will and prevail upon him to come on board the ship."

Omai repeated in Tahitian that they'd be safe. The white men were their friends.

A rope was thrown down from the ship to the natives in the canoe. A few of the men grabbed hold but still refused to come aboard. Ledyard looked down and saw one of the natives make funny faces up at the white sailors. Someone burst into laughter. In spite of the strangeness of the white men's ship, faces, manners, and speech, the laughter sounded familiar and somehow seemed to reassure the natives.

Cook lowered a pinnace into the water and went bravely ashore with a few marines for protection. He was immediately surrounded by curious swimmers, who tried to steal anything they could reach inside the boat. Ledyard and the others aboard the *Resolution* watched as their fellow marines beat back the natives, who were nearly upsetting the boat. Cook managed to return safely to the *Resolution.* He climbed on board, accompanied by an anxious native who had been chosen by Cook to pilot them to safe harbor. It was soon clear, however, that no safe landing place existed—except for outrigger canoes.

This was the second native Ledyard met who, like the Tasmanians, had never encountered white men. The bearded man named Mourua wore his dark hair drawn up in a topknot. He had an alert, bemused look about him. When Cook gave the man a knife, he hung it from his ear as an earring. The native was convinced to go below to Cook's cabin with much encouragement from Omai, the interpreter.

Everything fascinated the *Resolution* visitor—especially the strange animals on board. When he saw a goat, he turned to Omai and said something that made Omai laugh.

What was it? Cook demanded.

"He asked, 'What kind of bird is that?'" said Omai, who mistakenly trans-

Only one man from Mangaia (one of the Cook Islands), named Mourua, was brave enough to come aboard and have his portrait sketched. Mourua wore as an ear ornament the knife Cook gave him as a gift.

lated *manu* as "bird" rather than "animal." The crew, dependent on Omai's limited knowledge of the stranger's language, roared with laughter. Mourua good-naturedly had his portrait painted before he left the *Resolution*.

The ships circled the island and caught sight of more land, an island named Atiu, also previously undiscovered by Europeans. This island proved disappointing. The only way ashore seemed impossible. There was little fodder for the starving cattle. Coconuts, fish, and turtles were the main food available for the crew.

Three well-armed boats left the *Resolution* and made it close to the coral reef, where they were stopped by high surf. The only way across was to transfer to the waiting canoes of natives, who knew how to leap out of the way of the next breaker to avoid being overturned.

When the soggy group led by Omai as interpreter finally managed to land on shore, they were instantly surrounded by a growing throng of curiosity seekers. "They had not proceeded half a mile before they were plundered of every article they had about them," Ledyard said. The natives picked their pockets stealthily and robbed them openly.

When it was time to leave, the visitors discovered a party in progress. Omai nervously wondered whether the fire that was being prepared was to roast *them* rather than a pig. Fortunately, his fears proved groundless. Exhausted and hot, the visitors made it back to the ship unharmed—but still without the water or fodder they had hoped to discover.

Cook's disappointment and impatience showed. Not only had they wasted valuable time; they had also used up precious stores and water feeding the crew during the delay. The cattle were nowhere near being fed enough to survive, and it looked too dangerous to send any large group ashore to try and find grass.

At that very moment, he was supposed to be at latitude 45 degrees north— the coast of New Albion, now known as California—thousands of miles away. The ships cruised nearby Hervey Island, which Cook had visited on his last voyage. The island seemed deserted. The crew gathered whatever scurvy grass and coconuts they could find and fished with scoop nets.

Hervey Island and Palmerston Island, the next stop, were small, flat atolls. These atolls had sand or brittle coral-studded beaches, a few hardy trees, some birds, and perhaps fresh water. When populated, the islands' fragile environments had limited resources—something of little concern to Ledyard and the other men aboard the *Resolution.* For the natives who lived on atolls, the tension would be between how much the strangers would take and how much they would give away.

The pattern of discovery, contact, trade, theft, and misunderstanding would be repeated again and again. Each time the ships sailed away, Cook and his men had made as many enemies as friends.

On April 6 Cook made a decision that would have far-reaching consequences for the expedition. The search for the Northwest Passage would be delayed. He scrapped the timetable given to him by the Admiralty, because he was so disappointed in "all these islands" and the advanced season. "Summer in the northern Hemisphere already too far advanced for me to think of doing any thing there this year," Cook wrote. To preserve the cattle and what provisions they had left, they would instead go directly to the Friendly Islands, "where," Cook wrote, "I was sure of being supplied with every thing I wanted."

Cook relayed the message to Clerke in the *Discovery* and told him to open his sealed, secret instructions.

Naturally, when Ledyard and the others found out about their destination, they were delighted. They had heard stories about the Friendly, or Tonga, Islands, where the women were beautiful and welcoming and food was in abundance. They did not have to face the cold of the north but could linger longer in paradise.

On April 28 at nine o'clock in the morning, Ledyard and the rest of the crew spotted three small islands covered with trees and edged by white sandy beach. The sea broke some distance off each end. Then, like mysterious birds, three or four more islands came into view. The islands surrounded them as they tacked standing to the northeast.

By nightfall, the *Resolution* had signaled to the *Discovery* to anchor in a bay that was filled with coral sand and bits of shell. It wasn't long before canoes paddled closer and closer without hesitation. The canoes bartered breadfruit, plantains, yams, birds, citrus fruit called shaddocks, hogs, and fodder in exchange for pieces of cloth, fishhooks, small hatchets, and beads.

As word spread of the return of "Toot," as Cook was called by the islanders who first met him on an earlier voyage in 1774, the traffic became more brisk. The *Resolution* and the *Discovery* moved among the lovely islands with names like Kao and Tofua. Everywhere they went, they were swarmed by canoes filled with men and women, all trading eagerly.

Finally, on May 2, Cook and his officers and scientists went ashore with Ledyard and several of the other marines as guards to help gather wood and water. Huts were set up for the astronomer. Any bartering was strictly regulated by the gunner, whose job was to buy enough provisions for the ships. It was an exhilarating moment for Ledyard—"the first opportunity we had . . . of a free intercourse with the natives."

Every day there were concerts with music and dancing. Drums and bamboo instruments accompanied men who sang in a single voice, slow and solemn, while women marched. After a while the tempo picked up and so did the dancing, "as if the devil drove them," wrote First Lieutenant Burney, fascinated by the music's effect.

The ships continued to cruise the islands for the next several days. The crew went ashore to trade for food, cut firewood, and gather water. In early June, Ledyard was standing guard with several of his men on shore when Omai, proud and drunk, came up to the group. Words were exchanged. Omai struck one of the marines.

Ledyard pushed Omai away and threatened to beat him. Omai was insulted and humiliated. He considered himself a great man in the presence of these other islanders. Ledyard, showing his temper, had few endearing words for the overbearing traveler. After months in close quarters with Omai, whom he described as having "a proud empty ambitious heart," now was his chance to vent his spleen.

Omai, seizing the dramatic possibilities of the moment, marched to his tent, gathered up the two young New Zealanders, and went to one of the local chiefs. He stomped away and had a message sent to Cook. Omai intended, he said, "to return no More to the Ships." Revenge was what he had in mind.

Cook sent a message back to Omai and told him to return the next day, "& matters were made up to his satisfaction, tho' Captn Cook would not punish the Corporal as Omai had struck him while upon duty," wrote Surgeon's First Mate David Samwell. That seemed for the time to be the end of the unpleasantness.

The island was exceedingly beautiful and the weather "almost constantly fair." For Ledyard, this interlude in Tonga would be his first chance to experience Polynesian culture and politics. It seemed like paradise. On June 11, he and the other marines carried large tents ashore to serve as the astronomer's observatories. The livestock—four horses, several head of cattle, sheep, goats, hogs, peacocks, turkeys, and geese—were brought to shore and penned.

The natives found the horses and cattle frightening. It took quite a while for them to become accustomed to their size, noise, and motions. The ani-

The crowd cheered when Tongan stick combat contestants entered the ring.

mals' appearance, said Samwell, "excited as much astonishment and admiration as a Collection of wild Beasts at a Country Fair in England."

The encampment became a kind of marketplace, fairgrounds, and games arena. Natives from the island set up their own houses nearby. The spacious green was encircled by a grove of tall trees, wrote Ledyard. Near their encampment was a beautiful blue lagoon. From the beach he had a complete view of the two ships at anchor.

Cook, who had experienced problems with local trade before, immediately set up the rule that no sailor would be allowed to "traffick with the natives according to their own caprice," which usually meant trading a nail for the favors of a woman. Instead, only certain crew members were allowed to manage the trade on board and on shore. There was always the fear that overeager sailors might trade away all the beads, nails, and mirrors that might be needed to purchase future provisions. But there was no way to prevent the natives from swimming out into the harbor and swarming the ships.

One of the local chiefs, a middle-aged man named Polahow, "excessive fat . . . yet active and full of life," was invited on board by Cook, who found him "a Sedate sensible man." He was attended by another subchief named Phenow. Ledyard described Phenow as "one of the most graceful men I ever saw in the Pacific ocean." He was handsome, tall, and enterprising, "full of vivacity," who mostly kept on the move between the islands drumming up business—and, Cook would later learn, intrigue.

Ledyard described them both as "two noble Indians" and was impressed by the way they were able to keep the people under control during furious bargaining. Phenow's wife, "the most beautiful brunette for a wife that the

When Cook arrived at Nomuka, a marketplace was set up to trade glass beads, cloth, and items made of iron for coconuts, pigs, breadfruit, and yams.

hands of nature ever finished," also made a favorable impression on Ledyard. Using Omai as translator, Polahow asked astute questions that surprised Cook. What brought you to these islands? What is your business here? Where did you come from?

Cook showed him a map and was amazed that the "primitive" leader seemed to understand what he was saying. When Cook suggested that Polahow go below to his cabin, his attendants balked. Tradition said that no one's foot could be higher than the head of royalty. If Polahow went below deck, someone might walk overhead. Cook solved this by setting up an area on deck where no one could walk while he and the chief were in his cabin.

When it was Polahow's turn to show Cook hospitality, he invited the captain to shore. Cook came and tried, through Omai, to tell Polahow that he forbade any natives to steal from them. Cook then sent Ledyard and a few men around to march in formation as a show of force. Unfortunately, it was a rather undisciplined performance. At sunset Cook left and went back to the ship.

The evening was warm, the wind calm. Overhead a full moon shone. Nearby waves lapped the beach. The air was filled with the sweet smells of bougainvillea and hibiscus. Ledyard, stationed on shore, was surprised to find himself invited to Polahow's hut for dinner—a rather remarkable honor considering that Polahow was surrounded at any given moment by a sizable number of attendants. He crossed the clearing to the place where Polahow had his own temporary hut constructed.

Ledyard was invited inside. An attendant approached Polahow, squatting on the ground. He put Polahow's foot to his forehead, a sign of obedience. The attendant rose and left. When he returned, he carried a woven basket with fish cooked in plantain leaves, along with baked yams and a large coconut shell with fresh water. When Ledyard requested regular salt, an Indian fetched it for him. Ledyard ate heartily.

Polahow's attendants poured water on his hands while he washed them. They peeled his cooked yam, picked the bones from the fish, and fed him, "one putting Fish in his Mouth the other Yam." When dinner was finished, Polahow announced that it was time to sleep. He ordered his attendants to

Polahow, the highest-ranking man in Tonga, was described as "good natured and humane" by Ledyard.

unroll two large mats on the floor of the open hut. Small, wooden stool-like objects were used as pillows. Bolsters of cloth lay at the end of each mat.

Polahow lay on the mat. His attendants covered him with the cloth. He motioned for Ledyard to sleep nearby.

"Suddenly," Ledyard wrote, "I heard a number of their flutes beginning nearly at the same time." As Ledyard wondered if the music was supposed to be a lullaby, a seventeen-year-old girl appeared. "I must confess my heart suggested other matters," Ledyard admitted. The girl was Polahow's servant, who gave him his *tukituki*, or massage. "An extraordinary operation," Ledyard wrote. The girl patted plump Polahow with gentle strokes until he went to sleep. The massage, Ledyard later learned, seemed to help the chief's asthma.

Ledyard rose from his mat in "a listless reverie" and wandered out into the middle of the open area. The moon was shining down on him. The air was filled with flute music. Ledyard had a remarkable insight. For the first time he felt a kind of peace. Why was it, he wondered, that of all the animals in creation man was "the most happy and the most wretched, dancing through life between these two extremes, he sticks his head among the stars, or his nose in the earth." Perhaps he was describing himself when he wrote that man was "suspended by a cobweb in some middle altitude he hangs like a being indigenous to no sphere or unfit for any."

For Ledyard only the native, who "takes no pains to be happy"—the so-called Natural Man—can truly experience joy. At that moment Ledyard saw himself as part of the universe and yet at the same time as separate, an outsider looking in.

It was unfortunate that the blissful connection and mutual admiration could not continue throughout the rest of Cook's two-and-a-half-month visit. The islands seemed to embody a paradox. It was a land of plenty with easy weather and welcoming women. And yet at the same time, there was a definite hierarchy to the islands' ruling elite. There were internal politics, bristly and difficult to understand. And most of all, there was the pronounced need by the natives to take as much as they could from the white invaders.

Cook, who was accustomed to believing he always maintained the upper hand with the primitive people with whom he was trading, could not tolerate stealing. His men, of course, were becoming easy targets. The longer they stayed ashore, lulled by comfort and relaxation, the less attentive they became about watching the ships' belongings.

Except for gathering wood and water, there was little rigid routine to the seamen's days. They gave away too much. They got drunk. They fought.

It wasn't long before the "harmony" and understanding that Ledyard experienced on that moonlit night gave way to frequent thefts and misunderstandings on shore and on board ship. Second Lieutenant Phillips, the highest standing marine on the *Resolution*, claimed that all his bedding was stolen out from under him. Tools vanished from the carpenters' and sail makers' work site on shore. Wineglasses and goblets disappeared.

Cook's temper reached the boiling point. He tried disciplining his own men. Sleeping sentries were given a dozen lashes for neglect of duty. Thieves caught red-handed were treated with even greater cruelty: three dozen or even five dozen lashes. One man's arms were scored below the shoulder with a common knife. Thieves were fired at with small shot, painful but less lethal than actual balls.

These punishments had little effect. The natives simply pelted the shooters with rocks while hiding behind trees. On one occasion Cook had a thief's ear cut off, something he had never done before. George Gilbert, a young midshipman, found this especially offensive, "an act I cannot account for . . . than to have proceeded from a momentary fit of anger."

Ledyard also found Cook's actions strange. "Perhaps no considerations will excuse the severity which he sometimes used towards the natives on these occasions," Ledyard wrote. "And he would perhaps have done better to have considered that the full exertion of extreme power is an argument of extreme weakness."

Soon it was impossible for Ledyard or any other member of the crew to venture far into the island without being robbed or attacked.

On the evening of June 19, 1777, two prized turkey cocks and a young goat were stolen. The birds, Ledyard wrote, had been "brought from home at the expence of much care and trouble." Cook's temper skyrocketed. Using a technique that had successfully served him on other voyages, he seized three native canoes that happened to be floating beside the *Resolution.* Then he sent Ledyard and the other marines to surround Polahow's house in order to hold him and several other chiefs there for ransom. They would not be released, he said, until the birds and goat were returned.

This was an unpleasant job for Ledyard, who believed the chief to be innocent. All around Polahow's house, the people lamented and wept. The sounds of their cries disturbed Ledyard, who did not enjoy keeping guard on the bewildered Polahow. Meanwhile, Cook repeatedly demanded the return of the birds, which Ledyard claimed had been actually stolen by Phenow, who had disappeared.

People began to gather around the imprisoned chief's house. Cook told Polahow to order the growing crowd to leave. Polahow would be freed as soon as Cook's demands were met. The marines were ordered to draw their bayonets and point them at Polahow's enormous body. "This was too much," Led-

Tongan dancers performed with accompaniment from singers and rhythmic pounding of bamboo sticks.

yard said. Somehow Polahow managed to quell the growing crowd. That evening Polahow and the other chiefs went aboard the *Resolution* as prisoners.

The next day Phenow sent some swift canoes to Cook with the stolen birds and a quantity of red feathers, which were regarded of great trading value on other islands. Polahow was released, the other chiefs were freed, and the canoes were returned to their owners.

Polahow invited Cook and his men to an entertainment the following day. For the time being, Cook's wrath was forgotten. The evening was spent enjoying games, wrestling matches, dancing, and singing. Polahow and Phenow, dressed in splendid red- and yellow-feathered cloaks, marched into view.

Two enormous hogs were barbecued. Load after load of yams, breadfruit, plantains, shaddocks, and coconuts were heaped at Cook's feet. "We were fully convinced that we were strangers to the unbounded plenty of those happy islands," Ledyard wrote.

The marines from both ships were ordered to demonstrate marching in full uniform. Two French horns blared. Drums rolled. Flags waved. Ledyard and the others, who were certainly out of practice, performed in ragged formations along the beach.

Cook ordered a fireworks display to exhibit their military superiority. Unfortunately, the fireworks had been ruined by dampness aboard the *Discovery*. "They afforded little entertainment," Cook said. It was a disappointing event for the Tongans.

Completely dependent on the natives for food and water, Ledyard knew that he and the rest of the crew were demonstrating what was in fact only "imaginary superiority." They were outnumbered, and without their guns, their gunpowder, and the ability to load and fire, they could easily be massacred.

"Our only defence was certainly our imaginary greatness," Ledyard admitted. His comment proved prophetic. Little did he realize that a plot had been hatched by Phenow and several other chiefs to plunder the two ships and kill the crew during an evening of festivities in late May. Another English sea captain, who would visit Tonga thirty years later, discovered in interviews with Phenow's son and other chiefs that Ledyard and the rest of Cook's men owed their lives to the fact that at the last minute Phenow could not agree with the other chiefs on a plan of attack. The ambush fizzled like the dud fireworks.

In the months ahead the crew's "imaginary greatness" would continually be put to the test.

Chapter 6

UNACCOUNTABLE BEHAVIOR

From Tonga to Bora Bora
July–December 1777

After nearly three months in Tongatapu and the numerous other small islands that made up the Tonga, or Friendly, Islands, the natives' resources were so depleted that most of the people camped in temporary shelters on the beach near the ships had barely anything to eat. "Most of the yams [and other items] they brought with them were sold to us," Cook wrote.

It was time for the expedition to be on its way. What perplexed some of the officers was why Cook, the magnificent explorer, had not bothered during their long stay to take the time to explore and chart an island called Fiji that natives claimed was only three days' sail away. This island had not been explored or claimed by any European. "It is somewhat surprizing that Capt Cook did not go in search of it according to His usual practice," said Midshipman Gilbert. "His reasons for not doing it I can't account for; as we certainly had time while we were lying at Tongotaboo."

Ledyard could not have failed to hear about instances on Tongatapu in which his captain seemed to be behaving in other unaccountable ways. In July Cook had been invited to participate in a lengthy secret ceremony with the highest leaders of the island. At one point he was asked to leave. When he refused, the religious officials told him he had to "bare my shoulders as they were," Cook said. "With this I complied after which they seemed no longer uneasy at my presence."

Cook, always the model of proper dress in formal occasions, marched with the chiefs with his hair "hanging loose & his body naked down to ye waist," commented *Resolution* Third Lieutenant John Williamson, a righteous Irishman who irritated nearly everyone. "I cannot help thinking he rather let himself down."

In another perplexing gesture, Cook left behind in the Tonga Islands a horse, mare, bull and cow, and two goats. The men had struggled to keep this livestock alive for Omai's new home in Tahiti. Why had Cook suddenly disregarded King George's plan and jettisoned the animals before they reached their rightful home?

Most disturbing of all, however, was Cook's increasingly frequent rage. His punishment of natives and crew members became extreme. Anderson said he "scarcely . . . found [the captain's actions] consonant with the principles of justice or humanity." Aboard ship the captain was the law. His word decided everything. However, officers and sailors accustomed to Cook the compassionate leader on earlier voyages found his ruthless acts of violence alarming.

When the *Resolution* and *Discovery* set sail July 17, 1777, the people of the Tonga Islands were undoubtedly glad to see them go. Ledyard himself felt a kind of bittersweet regret in seeing the last of Phenow and Polahow, whose nobility made the white "civilized" crew seem to him "more savage themselves with all their improvements."

The next leg of the voyage proved to be a difficult passage—four weeks of rough weather. A hard gale carried away the *Discovery*'s main topmast and sprang her mainmast.

Finally, on August 12, land came into view. Tahiti, one of eight jewels called the Society Islands, loomed on the horizon. Cook had visited this paradise three years earlier. Silhouetted with jagged sawtooth mountain ridges, the islands of white beaches and green valleys assumed a kind of dreamlike quality. They were indeed among the most striking and beautiful of the places that Ledyard had yet visited.

The Society Islands were home to Omai and an estimated ten thousand natives. They were also a place where Cook, or "Tootee" as he was called there, was famous. As soon as the *Resolution* and *Discovery* anchors dropped in Mataivai Bay, excited native paddlers arrived and swarmed the ship. Their news, translated by Omai, was startling. Two strange ships with white men had visited the bay after Cook's last visit in 1774. They had built a house and a large wooden cross. They had left behind two religious men, a boy servant, an interpreter, and some livestock. The natives said they came from a place called "Rima," which Cook believed meant Lima, Peru.

Cook's beloved Tahiti had been claimed as a colony by the Spanish.

Although the Admiralty had forbidden him to interfere with or land in any country claimed by Spain, Cook hurried to shore. The Spanish friars had departed by ship after staying less than a year. What made Cook even more upset was when he discovered how much the natives admired the Spanish. The Tahitians were impressed that the Spanish forbade their men to mix with native women. The Spanish did not allow unfair bartering and punished their own people who "offered any injustice to the natives."

The Tahitians' feelings toward these other Europeans seemed to offer "proof that tender treatment may sometimes effect more than the force of arms," Anderson confided in his journal.

On the evening of August 14, Ledyard and the rest of the *Resolution* crew assembled to hear officially what many of them may have guessed all along: the true goal of the expedition. Cook assembled the ship's company and told them that they were searching for the Northwest Passage. He informed them that because of the distance involved and the season lost, their grog supply would not last and urged them to go half-ration—or even go without. The prospect of a huge monetary prize divided into shares and a vacation in paradise was enough to fill the crew with enthusiasm. Who needed grog?

The next several weeks were spent cruising the Society Islands, gathering supplies and visiting with various old friends. Tahiti seemed to Ledyard and the others a kind of lagoon-studded Eden filled with rich woods and jagged, picturesque mountains. "We were immediately surrounded by the inhabitants in their canoes, and the little village within the bay was full of people dancing and runing about with joy at our arrival," Ledyard wrote.

From the shore came the excited shouts of "Tootee! Tootee!"

Ledyard described the friendly inhabitants as "a very fine people, exceeding in beauty, in stature, strength, and the improvements of their mental capacities." He was especially impressed by the women. Everywhere the ships moored, the natives seemed "almost frantic with joy." Some of the sailors and marines, like Ledyard's superior, Sergeant Gibson, were fluent in the Tahitian language. Ledyard, fascinated by native culture, undoubtedly found himself in good company with Gibson, who was "always a very great favorite with the Indians."

Ledyard watched as Tahitians mobbed the ship to embrace old acquaintances with "the greatest affection." There was something odd and familiar about the homecoming. His fellow sailors seemed to be "as much and perhaps more pleased," he said, "than if they had been moored in any part in Great-Britain."

The marines rowed ashore to set up and guard the tents that would be home for the astronomer and his assistant. Carpenters, sail makers, and water gatherers went to work immediately.

The countryside was amazingly fertile. Breadfruit, coconuts, bananas "of thirteen sorts," Ledyard noted, as well as yams, sugarcane, and a kind of fruit that resembled an apple, abounded. On land were tame dogs, cats, hogs, and poultry. The sea was filled with fish. It was a land of plenty—a continuation of the idyll that the men had enjoyed in the Friendly Islands. Ledyard admitted that he found the people "extremely indolent, and sleeping and eating is almost all they do."

In the next several months, Ledyard had plenty of chances to observe the Tahitians closely. He visited their simple, elegant homes with thatched palm-leaf roofs and floors covered with dry grass. He ate their food, including cooked dog, which was baked in an underground pit. He watched their dances and wrestling and boxing matches. He tried to understand their religion, which he realized was impossible, since he claimed the Tahitians lied. Indeed communication was a problem since beside Gibson and a few others, the only person who spoke fluently was Omai, a man who often used his knowledge and observations to his own best advantage.

Ledyard became so infatuated with the Tahitians that, like many of his fellow sailors, he had his hands tattooed. The custom of "staining their bodies," he said, "is universal among all these islands." This was done by pricking the skin with an instrument made from a small sharp bone dipped in a mixture of coal dust and water, which leaves an indelible stain. "The operation is painful," he admitted, "and it is some days before the wound is well."

Why he decided to have his hands tattooed he never explained. It may have confirmed his sense of belonging to the rest of the company—or perhaps of some wildness he wished to take away with him as a reminder. Whatever the reason, the tattoos would "mark" him for life. They were an obvious, unconcealable mark of his experience in an exotic, faraway place.

Ledyard went as far as to try and learn the language, which he compared with what he had learned of the New Zealand tongue. He wondered if the South Sea Island people originated from the same place and spread thousands of miles into new islands—some nearly four thousand miles apart.

An aimless lethargy took hold of the crew. Without enough to do to keep occupied, they soon found themselves quarreling. Lieutenant Williamson and Marine Lieutenant Phillips fought an abortive pistol duel over an argument about the marines' inefficiency. Other crew members became so enamored of their new surroundings, they went "native," tossing off their old clothes and old ways. It was tempting. The Tahitians were among the most friendly and amiable of those they had encountered, and the women were "in fact angels," *Discovery* Master Thomas Edgar wrote, later claiming that his time in Tahiti was "the happiest three months I ever spent."

For Cook, any sense of order and control over his own men seemed to be slipping away. The ship crawled with cockroaches that ate everything in sight. Bold rats scrambled everywhere. It was impossible to smoke and fumigate regularly. There were women on board every night. Crew members fell asleep on watch. They got into drunken quarrels with one another. It was the same story he had seen in the Friendly Islands—only worse.

The Society Islands were achingly beautiful: sapphire-blue water, lagoons

An arioi *dance-drama was performed for Cook's crew by skilled actors and pantomime artists in Otaheite (now known as Tahiti).*

with white sand beaches, palm trees rustling in the soft tropic breezes. The land itself arched up like the setting of some medieval fairy tale. Scattered among jagged-toothed mountains covered with greenery and volcanic black peaks, were lush valleys that caught light and tempted the eye with impossible distance.

For Ledyard, the three-month idyll in the Society Islands was filled with contradictions. On the one hand, he enjoyed every pleasure available. He admired the women, the food, the weather. And yet even among so much ease, something nagged him. His ambition.

The blue-green sea lapped at Ledyard's feet. Whispering. This was Cook's third visit to Tahiti. He had thoroughly charted the coasts. There was nothing new, nothing exciting to be discovered here. How could someone as ambitious as Ledyard prove himself heroic in a place where the most exciting event was yet another dance or feast, called a *heiva*? After so many weeks of

Craggy peaks soar above Oitapeeah Bay in this inland view of the island of Otaheite, by William Ellis.

languor, Ledyard may have begun to wonder if he would have the strength or nerve enough for grand heroic action.

On October 6, Cook announced that they were leaving Tahiti and heading northwest a few miles to the smaller, heart-shaped island of Moorea—a place that proved to be even more beautiful than Tahiti. The sailors unwillingly went through the motions of their duties reloading the ship. They said good-bye to their sweethearts. Some of the women stayed aboard. Others followed in their own canoes.

No one could have predicted that the most beautiful of places would become the scene of some of the worst violence. And it all began with a goat.

On October 7, the two ships were anchored near Moorea. In this new location there were fewer people on shore. Perhaps Cook thought there would be fewer temptations. Unfortunately, there was also less control. The chiefs did not rule with the iron fist of their Tahitian counterparts. Thefts by natives began almost immediately.

Tents were set up for the astronomer. Wood- and water-gathering parties were sent out. Cattle was brought ashore to feed. The regimen was the same as always. And yet in spite of the beauty of their surroundings, something was wrong. Very wrong.

Unlike most of his men, Cook did not enjoy leisure. He had never in his life been so far behind schedule in accomplishing an expedition's goals. After fifteen months at sea, he was nowhere near the point he was supposed to be. Cook knew that, unlike on his previous expeditions, another ship would be waiting to connect with his at the end of the voyage.

Yet here he was in Moorea, a place he had already visited twice before. He was covering no new terrain, charting no new lands. With every wasted day, his provisions had to be replenished. He knew he did not have enough grog to supply his crew. Trade supplies such as axes, nails, and beads—which could not be restocked—were being steadily depleted.

Worse yet, he could see his own men begin to dissipate. The "venereals," as he called venereal disease, had taken a toll that disheartened him. Even more discouraging was watching the collapsing health of his most trusted crew members: Clerke, Anderson, and loyal old Watman, the forty-five-year-old able seaman. Clerke and Anderson had incurable tuberculosis. Watman was wasting away with an unknown disease. How long would they last?

Ledyard and the others may not have sensed their captain's growing impatience and anxiety at first. Cook seemed all right as he attended local leaders and gave away such gifts as hatchets, red feathers, and linen dressing gowns printed with large flowers. But as soon as the trading ceremony was completed and the natives left, Cook noticed that a goat, sent ashore to feed with the rest of the livestock, was missing. Why, he fumed, some ungrateful *tito* (a word Cook picked up on earlier travels that he took to mean thief) had had the temerity to swipe one of his animals!

There was nothing particularly precious about goats. Unlike much larger horses, bulls, or cows, which had been transported at much expense of time and effort, goats were hardy. They came cheap. And yet when this particular goat vanished from the shore, Cook was furious. On such a small ship, his anger could be felt by everyone around him.

Cook sent several marines ashore armed with deadly shot. Their mission was to deliver the local chief a threat in an attempt to get the goat back. While the boat was en route, another goat—this one pregnant—vanished from shore.

This was the last straw. Cook demanded Omai's advice. The wily Tahitian, always eager for any kind of bloody revenge, suggested taking a party of men into the country and "shooting Every Soul" they encountered.

On October 8, the few inhabitants who lived near the shore where the ships were moored quietly slipped away. They could sense something was brewing. Something awful. So could Ledyard and the rest of the marines. The goat was no longer a simple innocent animal. It had become the symbol of native defiance of Cook's supreme, civilizing European authority. Didn't the Tahitians realize that they were puny and worthless? Didn't they know they were primitive and powerless?

At daybreak the next morning, Cook ordered every marine from both ships, plus the "gentlemen"—a total of thirty-five armed men—accompanied by a local guide and the excitable Omai, to march across the island to the place where the local head chief, Mahine, reportedly was living. Mahine had been fingered as the thief. Meanwhile, three armed boats under the direction of Lieutenant Williamson were rowed around to the western part of the island.

Cook marched his men in hot, humid weather over sharp, brittle volcanic rocks. Each terrified native they encountered begged for mercy. Each, when told they would not be killed, informed Cook that the goat had been moved, always just out of reach.

When they finally reached a few houses, men darted out of sight in the trees, carrying darts, spears, and clubs. The houses were mostly empty. When Cook told the few remaining inhabitants that if he didn't get his goat back, he'd begin burning their homes, the people acted as if they had no idea what he was talking about. A goat? What goat?

The Resolution *and* Discovery *anchored at Eimeo in Moorea. In the middle foreground marines help unload cargo. This scene was sketched by James Clevely and later painted by his brother, John.*

Cook ordered Ledyard and the rest of the marines to light torches. They set fire to six or eight houses. Ledyard watched the houses become enveloped in flames—all the owners' belongings destroyed. Woven mats crackled and turned black. Smoke filled the air. Ledyard and the other marines shifted nervously from foot to foot. Only days before, they had enjoyed the pleasures of hospitality in such homes, the easy friendship of people who invited them in to share their food, their drink, and their women. Maybe this would be all. Maybe the captain meant just a warning. Nothing more.

No, Cook announced. They weren't finished. Destroy their canoes.

The canoes?

Three large war canoes, painstakingly created and measuring forty-five feet in length, were hacked to splinters. Such destruction was a sorry task for the sailors, who knew how much work went into the sleek vessels. The canoes were the natives' most prized possessions and their sole means of transport from island to island.

This done, Cook marched his bewildered men off to join the boats. On their way, they burned six more war canoes. No native stopped them. No one came out of hiding. The ease of destruction began to appeal to some of the men. Why not pillage while they were at it? Why not kill a few dogs and rough up the hogs a bit? It wasn't long before the unruly, dark side of the tars took over. After weeks of doing nothing, they seemed to enjoy destruction. They burned *tapa,* cloth made from pounded bark. They smashed bowls and gourds. The more the men sacked and ravaged, the more excited they became.

Ten or twelve native men appeared, waving plantain leaves as signs of peace. They laid these at the soldiers' feet. They begged and groveled for their canoe to be spared.

Godlike Cook, feeling magnanimous, paused. Not this one, he indicated. And the canoe went unharmed.

That evening there was still no returned goat. "All I had yet done had not had the desired effect," Cook complained. The next morning, another threat was sent to the chief named Mahine. If he didn't send the goat, Cook would demolish every canoe on the island. To show the messenger he meant business, he had the carpenters break up three or four canoes on shore—wood that would be later used to build Omai's ill-fated house.

Ledyard and the rest of the marines were ordered to destroy everything—houses, cultivated fields, hogs, dogs, canoes. Smoke rose. There were sounds of lamentation from the natives. Screams of women. No one enjoyed the forty hours of chaos and fires and plunder more than Omai, who greedily raced about from house to house gathering up whatever he could salvage for himself. Others joined him in plundering souvenirs.

No natives were killed or hurt, although, as Midshipman George Gilbert confessed, they probably would have been had they shown the least resistance.

An outrigger canoe similar to the ones Cook's crew destroyed on Moorea. This sketch was made by John Webber.

For someone like Ledyard, there was nothing heroic in these actions. He was forced to follow orders, just like the other marines. Cook "seemed very rigid in the performance of his Orders which everyone executed with the greatest reluctance," Gilbert said. To refuse would have meant a severe flogging. Even for someone as vindictive as the irritating Lieutenant John Williamson, the order seemed repulsive. "I must confess this once," he wrote, "I obey'd my Orders with reluctance."

What was most disturbing for the men who were repulsed by the violence was what they saw happening to their beloved leader. What was wrong with Cook? No one who had sailed with him before had ever seen him act with such pitiless violence toward native people. Instead of a brief "*heiva*," as they called his increasingly frequent stomping temper tantrums, Cook's anger had boiled over into two days of burning and pillaging.

"I can't well account for Captain Cook's proceedings on this occasion as they were so very different from his conduct in like cases in his former voyages," confided Gilbert. Second Lieutenant James King agreed. He could not find anything justifiable about what he called "the depredations." He added, "In the future they may fear, but never love us."

On October 11, unloved and unwanted, the men from Cook's ships took back the wayward stolen goat and set sail for another Society Island, this one called Huahine, one hundred miles west of Tahiti. This was to be the place where Omai would set up his new home, since it was clear he would never be welcome at Moorea. Omai followed Cook in his large war canoe, which was overloaded with plunder, and which he had aptly named *Royal George* after the king of England. The *Royal George* had been purchased for Omai by Cook in happier days in Tahiti before their troubles began.

News of Cook's destruction multiplied ten times by the time the ships arrived in Huahine. The natives seemed nervous in their welcome, as if they wondered when the white men would finally be gone for good. "I had hopes they would behave a little better than they usually had done at this island," Cook wrote with little remorse.

Omai came ashore in a strange combination of clothing that Ledyard found amusing. He wore a shining armor breastplate over his Tahitian toga. On his head was a Tongan red-feathered cap. He bestowed presents of red feathers upon those he wished to impress. No one seemed suitably overwhelmed, according to Cook.

In spite of the chilly reception, Cook purchased some land for Omai. Using planks from the Mooreans' destroyed canoes, and with as few nails as possible to discourage stealing, the crew built Omai a 24-by-18-foot house with a 10-foot-tall ceiling. They planted a proper English-style garden. They stocked the house with Omai's toys from England—his jack-in-the-box, drums, organ, electrifying machine, compass, gloves, sea charts, and toy soldiers. They unloaded his arsenal of guns and his pots, kettles, and pewter dishes for housekeeping.

Omai demonstrated horseback riding before a crowd of natives. (He fell off almost immediately.) He tried to impress his new neighbors with target practice and fireworks. He had a pet monkey that the natives called "Oroo Tat," or Hairy Man, a boar, two sows of the English breed, a mare, and eight servants including the two New Zealand youths, Coaa and Tiarooa.

The move to his new house seemed to be going along rather peacefully until October 25, when someone stole from the astronomer's tent the sextant used to take navigational bearings. This equipment was irreplaceable.

Cook interrupted a *heiva* and theatrical performance and collared the thief, who was sitting casually in the crowd. Omai insisted that this was the man responsible. Immediately, the rest of the audience panicked and ran away—terrified that they would meet with the revenge that had been experienced on Moorea. Rumor was that this was the same man responsible for tearing up Omai's garden.

Cook ordered the thief to be brought on deck and have his head shaved and both ears cut off—an operation that was stopped at the last moment by Second Lieutenant James King. The man was kept captive until he suddenly disappeared overboard on October 30, when a marine who was supposed to be guarding him fell asleep. Omai's sworn mortal enemy, the man who had promised to burn his house and kill him, was now on the loose.

Furious, Cook punished the entire watch, who had *all* fallen asleep on deck. Both the mate and the midshipman of the watch were lowered in rank. The midshipman was turned before the mast, which meant he became a common seaman and lost all the privileges available to officers. The sentinel and quartermaster were kept in irons and flogged every day for three days. Rumors circulated that the thief was let go on purpose by someone among the crew.

It was too late to search for him now. The ships needed to be on their way. On November 2, Cook's men fired a five-gun salute. Omai cried pitifully. But the most moving of all to Ledyard and the others aboard were the reactions of the two boys from New Zealand. They had become great favorites of the crew, who had taught them little amusing routines and jokes and bits of English. Distraught Coaa, the younger of the two, dived into the water and tried to swim to the *Resolution*. The ship sailed quickly out of reach. Natives in a canoe rescued the boy and brought him back to shore.

A view of Huahine, where the ships' carpenters built a wooden house for Omai.

When the ships reached Bora Bora, another island, *Resolution* Marine Private John Harrison took his gun and disappeared into the jungle. His desertion was followed by two more from the *Discovery:* Midshipman A. Mouat and Thomas Shaw, gunner's mate. All three were in love with local girls. They knew the ships were headed for the perilous arctic. Sensing that they might never return, they decided to escape with supplies into paradise. Ledyard wrote glowingly of their escape and capture, which cost the ships another week of delay.

Cook used one of his earlier tactics to have the men returned: he held several chiefs of Bora Bora for ransom. Ledyard, perhaps echoing the earlier threats, wrote: "If [the chief] did not aid and assist in procuring his men . . . he would come with his ships and destroy him and his people without mercy." The men were found and brought back to the ship. They were all reduced in rank and punished. The ransomed chiefs were let go, Ledyard wrote, "and were as fully convinced of our future friendship as if this cause which had interrupted it had never happened."

It was not until December 8, 1777, that they finally lifted anchor. Ledyard and the other marines turned the capstan and sang sorrowfully with the other sailors:

O, the times are hard and the wages low
Leave her, Johnny, leave her
I'll pack my bag and go below
It's time for us to leave her.

Ledyard was as depressed as anyone aboard the *Resolution* or the *Discovery* as the islands faded from view. "We left these Islands with the greatest regret immaginable," Midshipman George Gilbert confided. "And supposing all the pleasure of the voyage to be now at an end; having nothing to expect in future but excess of cold, hunger, and every kind of hardship and distress attending a Sea Life in General and these voyages in particular, the idea of which rendered us quite dejected."

Health worries probably plagued Ledyard and the rest of the crew as they began their journey northward. The only trained doctor, William Anderson, was suffering from the last stages of tuberculosis. On board the *Discovery,* Captain Clerke had become so weak that he seldom appeared above deck. The oldest man on the expedition second to Cook, forty-five-year-old William Watman of the *Resolution,* was also failing. The able seaman, who had a twenty-one-year career in the navy, had served with Cook on his previous voyage. Everyone knew that Cook viewed Watman as a kind of good luck charm. Among the superstitious crew, Watman's illness did not bode well for the voyage.

If Cook was worried about Anderson, Clerke, or Watman, he kept his thoughts to himself. Always a private man, he did not reveal to anyone his concerns about his own health. Little did he realize that the strange swings in his mood and appetite could be traced to the Society Islands. Some medical experts believe that it was here three years earlier that Cook probably acquired an illness that was beginning to devastate his physical and mental well-being. Roundworms, which thrived in undercooked or rancid Tahitian pork, had infested his intestine. This tropical parasite slowly caused his body to be unable to absorb vitamin B. The result? Fatigue, depression, loss of concentration and memory, and personality changes—all of which could have devastating consequences for the expedition.

Chapter 7

A NEW DISCOVERY

From Bora Bora to Hawaii
December 1777–January 1778

For the next three weeks, the *Resolution* and *Discovery* headed north and north-west. At dawn on a tropical Christmas Eve, 1777, Ledyard and the other men sailed toward a small speck on the mid-Pacific no one had ever charted before.

"Land!" the lookout called.

The uninhabited, barren-looking island did not seem promising. Another coral atoll ringed by a reef and high surf. Cook named it Christmas Island and sent two sloops ashore to find a safe place to land. "This is a low, small island," Ledyard wrote, "mostly of coral rock, and scarcely more than 15 feet above the surface of the water in the highest part of it."

The men went ashore to hunt down fresh water and anything green to eat. Tents were set up for the astronomer to observe an eclipse of the sun, which was predicted to occur on December 27. On a hot Christmas Day, Cook allowed the men double allowance of liquor and a feast of fresh pork and fish. It was an evening of "mirth and jollity," one of Bligh's mates wrote.

Nothing marred the day of "revels," not even the fact that the island was surrounded by more sharks than Ledyard had ever seen before. Flocks of seabirds and enormous green turtles—some weighing as much as one hundred pounds—also cruised around the island. Ledyard and the other men

COOK'S THIRD VOYAGE—
THE SOUTH PACIFIC (1777)

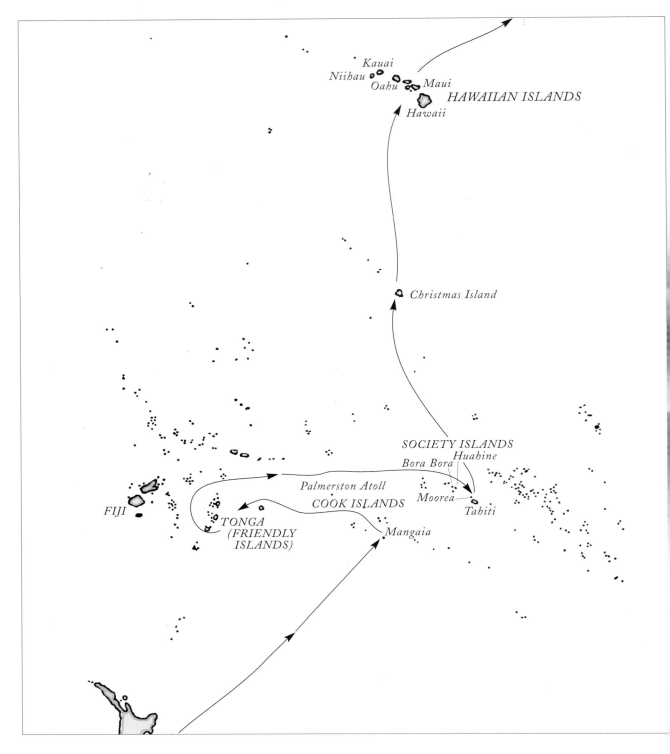

Kauai
Niihau
Oahu
Maui
Hawaii
HAWAIIAN ISLANDS

Christmas Island

SOCIETY ISLANDS
Huahine
Bora Bora
Palmerston Atoll
Moorea
COOK ISLANDS
Tahiti

FIJI

TONGA
(FRIENDLY
ISLANDS)

Mangaia

who knew how to swim went out into the lagoon in turtle-wrestling parties. They stayed inside the reef, where they hoped to be safe from sharks.

As soon as the tide went out and the clear water became shallow enough, Ledyard sloshed out knee deep and caught the turtles by the back flippers. With delight he was dragged into deeper water and the bucking bronco ride began. In half an hour Ledyard and the other men caught and corralled forty-two turtles—all of which were eventually eaten.

Ledyard knew his family was celebrating Christmas thousands of miles away. This was his second Christmas in a row away from home. He was as distant as he could possibly be from the world of cold New England wind and snow and disapproving relatives.

Before the *Resolution* and *Discovery* stood out to sea on January 2, 1778, Cook left behind a bottle containing a Latin inscription claiming the place for Britain. He ordered the men to plant a small patch of melon seeds to aid future wayward, hungry travelers.

The ships continued their journey north into a little-known area of the Pacific. Everyone expected cold, fierce weather ahead. Cries of seabirds echoed. Every so often a turtle darted past—all signs of land.

On the morning of January 18, an unexpected, mountainous island loomed in the distance. It was Oahu, one of the middle islands in a crescent-shaped string of islands now called the Hawaiian group. Directly ahead of the ship appeared Kauai, then to the west, Niihau. "This was immediately determined from our position to be a new discovery," Ledyard wrote, "and of course gave every one joy."

The men let out a loud whoop. After nearly eighteen months at sea, this was the expedition's most dramatic sighting yet—a significant landform that did not appear on any European map. The discovery of these green, promising islands in the boundless Pacific seemed once again to point to Cook's remarkable timing and good fortune.

The ships' approach seemed frustratingly slow for the excited crews. Ledyard studied the coast. He could make out surf and a strip of white sand beach. Occasionally smoke floated above the distant trees: a sign of inhabitants. As they grew closer, he could see people on shore—first a few, then a gathering crowd. Were they friendly? Or were they warlike cannibals?

"We had been approached several times by some canoes at a distance," Ledyard wrote, "but none of them would come near enough to converse with us or that we might see what sort of people they were." Canoes paddled closer. The natives, armed with rocks and spears, studied the big ships from a safe distance. "They appeared inexpressibly suprized, though not intimidated," Ledyard wrote. "They shook their spears at us, rolled their eyes about and made a variety of wild uncouth gesticulations."

Lieutenant Burney and Sergeant Gibson, both fluent in the Tahitian language, called down to the frightened visitors. "What is the name of your island?" "Is the fish good?" "Where are the women?"

"We found to our joy and surprise that with little variation their language was the same as that of our acquaintance at the southern islands," Ledyard wrote. The idea was at first amazing. "How shall we account for this nation having spread itself in so many detached islands, so widely disjointed from each other, in every quarter of the Pacific Ocean!"

Here indeed were sailors. The distance from Hawaii to New Zealand is 4,041 nautical miles. The nearest inhabited island, Tahiti, is 2,372 nautical miles away. The *Resolution* and *Discovery* were among the most sophisticated ships of their day. How had natives in simple, fragile outrigger canoes navigated and survived the journey? It seemed impossible.

On January 20, Cook invited a few islanders on board. Only the bravest ventured up onto the *Resolution.* They seemed astonished and overwhelmed. The natives were not as tall as the Tahitians, "but of strong, muscular make," Lieutenant James King wrote. "There was great variety in the shape of their visages."

"They were exceeding wild," Ledyard wrote. "[They] ran up to us and examined our hands and faces, then stripping up our shirt sleeves and opening the bosoms of our shirts to view such parts of our bodies as were covered by our cloaths."

The Hawaiians seemed never to have seen a white person before. Were these visitors even human? they may have wondered. Could they eat? The

One of hundreds of double-rigged canoes that greeted Cook and his crew in the Sandwich (now known as Hawaiian) Islands. These paddlers were depicted in masked helmets decorated with foliage and tassels of tapa, or cloth made from bark.

Only the most powerful Hawaiian chiefs wore the magnificent cap and cape made of hundreds of thousands of bright red and yellow feathers from rare birds.

sailors demonstrated by chomping a few biscuits. The natives called down to the paddlers in the canoes. Bring hogs! Bring potatoes! And soon a brisk trade began. "Several small pigs were got for a sixpenny nail," Cook wrote. A sixpenny nail was only one and a half inches long.

Thievery, Cook noted, began almost immediately. The first Hawaiian who came on board was there only a moment before he decided to take off with a lead and line. He gathered up his plunder and headed straight for his canoe. When he was caught, he simply turned and with a careless gesture seemed to imply, "Well, I am just going to put it in my boat." It was only when an officer found a Hawaiian who would try to stop him that the man put back what he'd stolen.

Meanwhile, Cook ordered Third Lieutenant John Williamson and the marines to look for a landing place. A Hawaiian grabbed the butcher's cleaver and leaped overboard, then swam to his canoe and escaped before anyone could stop him. "The third day after our arrival we went on shore and traded with them there, and viewed the country," Ledyard wrote.

Cook gave the crew strict orders not to allow women on board or to have any kind of connection with them. He was especially specific that "none who had the venereal upon them should go out of the ships." There were as many as sixty men on board, including Ledyard, who may have been suffering from venereal disease at the time.

Syphilis, a chronic venereal disease, had become a dangerous epidemic in Europe by the late eighteenth century. Communicated by sexual contact, the incurable disease, called "the pox," caused painful sores, disfigurement, blindness, insanity, and death. Mercury was the basic remedy, applied in huge quantities as an ointment, orally, and in vapor baths. Regularly breathing lethal doses of mercury fumes could cause severe mental disorders.

On Cook's earlier voyages to Tahiti and New Zealand, his men spread the disease among the native population. The men on the third expedition may have picked up the disease from women infected by this earlier contact.

Cook, Anderson, and many of the other officers were well aware of the tragedy of the spread of this incurable disease among unsuspecting populations. Anderson was especially harsh in his condemnation of the infected sailors who knowingly disregarded their condition and spread the disease among native women.

Since this was a completely new country, Cook tried his best to keep the contaminated men away from the natives. "Captain Cook prohibited all intercourse between us & the women, on acct of a number of our people not being free from the fowl disease, they got at the Society Islands which was a great disappointment to the Girls," wrote the *Discovery* astronomer William Bayly. Unfortunately, Cook's rules soon became impossible to enforce. Some of the sailors concealed their condition in order to get on shore. Others dressed women up as men to slip them on board.

Early in the morning of January 20, Williamson, who always seemed to be in the wrong place at the wrong time, went ashore with the first group

Trade began as soon as the crew arrived on the beach near the village of Waimea on the island of Kauai.

of marines to locate sources of fresh water. They were mobbed by eager Hawaiians, who nearly tipped their boat in a wild search for nails. The marines and the sailors tried to hold their guns above the surf and at the same time grip the oars. Williamson panicked and shot and killed one of the Hawaiians who tried to pull the boat hook.

"I just mention'd the orders I had given not to fire with out my directions, I repeat this in order to point out the necessity of giving such orders, from ye great wantonness of the inferior people on board a ship, & yet idea they posses that it is no harm to kill an indian," Williamson wrote revealingly in his journal.

The murdered Hawaiian was about forty years old, a "handsome man . . . & seemed to be a Chief," Williamson admitted. As soon as the Hawaiian plunged into the bloody water, the other natives rushed away. The men in the boat oared hard to back up and rush out of reach. Only later did the natives return to retrieve the body. Williamson avoided telling Cook what had happened. When Lieutenant Molesworth Phillips, Ledyard's superior, found out, he was outraged. Relations between Williamson and Phillips worsened.

It was a bad beginning.

Meanwhile, Cook had gone to shore in Kauai. The natives reacted with surprising awe. "The very instant I leaped ashore," Cook said, "they all fell flat on their faces, and remained in that humble posture till I made signs to them to rise." To the Hawaiians, Cook seemed to be a king. They piled the beach with small pigs without asking for anything in trade. Williamson, however, attributed the natives' groveling manner and generosity to the "good effects of at once shewing our superiority."

Ledyard and several other marines were sent ashore to act as guards during trading for ship supplies. A large crowd gathered, and a kind of market was set up on the beach: "a brisk trade for pigs, fowls and roots which was carried on with the greatest good order," Cook commented with satisfaction. A moderate-size nail provided enough pork for the ships' company. Casks were rolled on shore and filled with fresh water.

"We had nothing to fear from the natives," Cook wrote on January 21. Cook was treated to a tour of the village. Everywhere he, Anderson, and the ship's artist, John Webber, went, the natives dropped to the ground in obedient bows.

Ledyard saw that their arrival in new, uncharted territory was his chance to shine. He had become acquainted with *Resolution* First Lieutenant John Gore, who had also been born in America. Gore, an experienced sailor with thinning red hair and pale blue eyes, was the oldest officer on the voyage, second to Cook. Always the opportunist, Ledyard realized that the only way he'd get any attention was to attach himself to a superior.

On January 30, Gore took Ledyard and several other marines—a party of about twenty—ashore in a small boat to Niihau, the most western island. They were ordered to search for fresh water and, according to Cook, "to trade with the Natives for refreshments." A storm suddenly came up in the night. High surf pounded the beach and prevented the small party from returning to the *Resolution*. Communication was cut off.

"We traded with the natives at Nehow," Ledyard wrote.

That was not all they did.

In spite of Cook's orders, the "extreme reservedness of the party excited

Ledyard called First Lieutenant John Gore, born in Virginia, "my countryman." This portrait was created by Webber in 1780, when Gore was fifty years old.

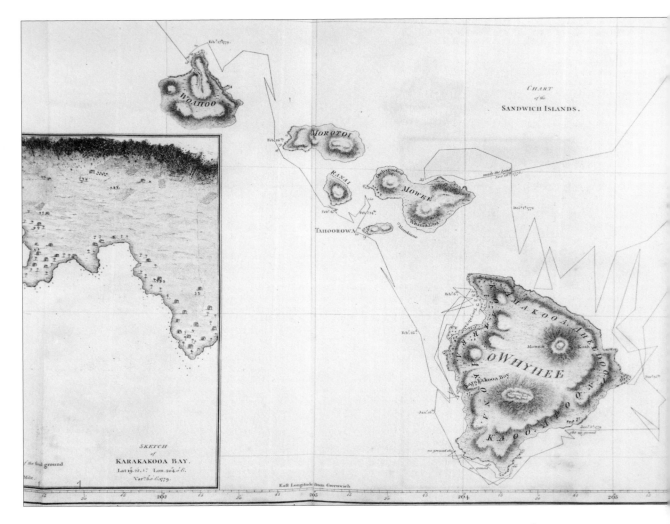

This map shows the path the ships took as they slowly circled the Sandwich (now known as Hawaiian) Islands—much to the impatience of the crew. (inset) Kealakekua Bay

so great a curiosity in the women, that they were determined to see wether our people were men or not, & us'd every means in their power to provoke them to do that, which ye dread of punishment would have kept them from," Third Lieutenant John Williamson confessed.

"Thus the very thing happened that I had above all others wished to prevent," Cook said with a sigh.

Food gathering on Niihau proved to be wasted effort. Most of the pork and plantains they had traded were lost when the boats overturned while trying to get back to the ship on February 1.

On January 27, Thomas Roberts, quartermaster on the *Resolution*, died of dropsy. "He had not done a week's duty since his Departure from England," Midshipman John Watts complained. That same night, the sergeant of the marines, Samuel Gibson, fell overboard. He was drunk and sleeping on the gangway. Someone had the presence of mind to throw out the newfangled lifesaving machine, which did not work very well because of high waves. He managed to save himself nonetheless.

"Our stay was short," Ledyard wrote wistfully of their visit to the place Cook would name the Sandwich Islands after his patron, the Earl of Sandwich. Sandwich, the first Lord of the Admiralty, had given Cook the command of the third voyage. He was the one whose signature adorned Cook's secret instructions. He was the same man who was said, according to tradition, to have invented the sandwich during a twenty-four-hour bout at the gaming table with no other refreshment than slices of cold beef between slices of toast.

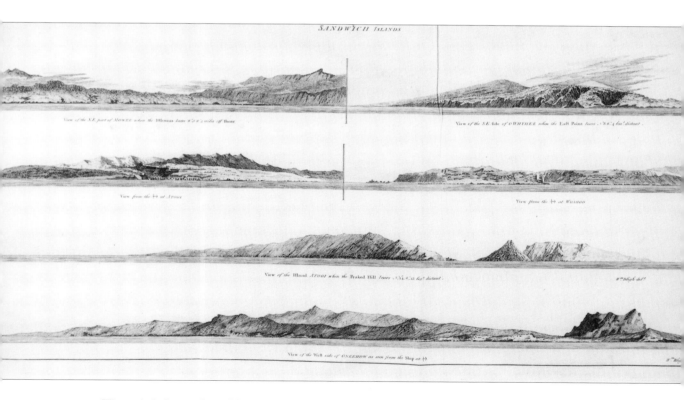

First sightings of the Hawaiian Islands were sketched by William Bligh.

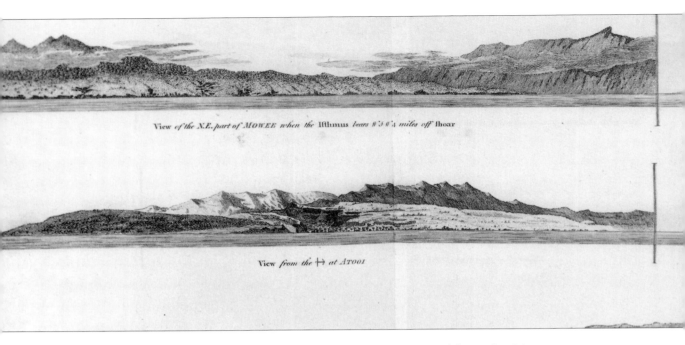

View of the N.E. part of MOWEE when the Isthmus bears N.S.W.4 miles off Shoar

View from the ⚓ at ATOOI

(above) The island of Maui as it appeared from the ship.
(below) The coast and mountains of Kauai

Of course it would have been pleasant to linger among the beautiful tropical islands, but time was growing short. Cook probably would have liked to have finished charting the new discovery, in spite of the difficult waters and uncooperative winds, but he knew there was only a small window of opportunity to explore the northern reaches of the coast of New Albion.

On February 2, 1778, Ledyard and the other sailors leaned into the capstans and helped lift the anchors of the *Resolution* and *Discovery*. "We again launched into that extensive ocean that separates America from Asia, and continued our course northward and eastward," Ledyard wrote. At the moment of their departure, they "close hauled with a gentle gale Easterly," Cook wrote. Neither he nor anyone else thought they would return to these islands. No one would have predicted that Cook's discovery would ultimately be his last anchorage.

Chapter 8

NORTHERN LIGHTS

From Hawaii to Nootka Sound
February–April 1778

Temperatures plummeted. During the next five weeks, Ledyard and the other seamen shivered with cold. On February 25, 1778, the northern night sky shimmered with the ghostly lights of the aurora borealis. When daylight returned, the crew was surprised to discover four-foot-long clumps of green rockweed and bobbing pieces of driftwood floating past the ships—hints of nearby land.

More strange signs appeared. On the night of March 1, the water suddenly filled with "a great number of little sparks . . . which Exhibited a Firy Light and swam about very briskly," wrote Gore. The next day the crew scooped up a bucket of water and discovered that the frisky stars they had seen were actually little animals "no bigger than wood lice" that Gore said "shone like bitts of bright silver."

On March 6, two seals swam past. Whales plunged near enough to the ship to be observed by Ledyard and the other sailors. At daybreak the next morning, "the long looked for Coast of new Albion was seen extending from NE to SE distant 10 or 12 leagues," Cook wrote with relief. The hilly land was covered with trees. Beyond loomed a flat-topped mountain, now known as St. Mary's Peak, on the Oregon coast.

Almost immediately upon reaching latitude 44 degrees 55 minutes north,

COOK'S THIRD VOYAGE—
ALASKAN EXPEDITIONS (1778 AND 1779)

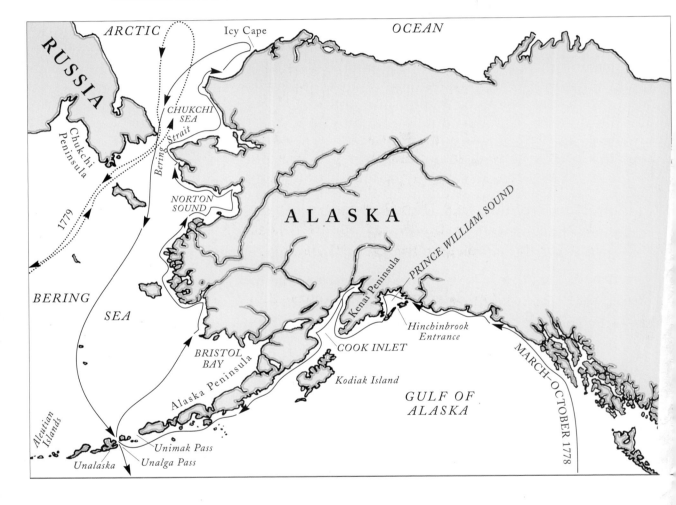

their glimpse of New Albion slid shut like a closed curtain. Bad weather slammed the ships. The crew could see nothing through gray clouds and wind-driven sheets of rain. It was, Ledyard said, the "ruggedest weather we had yet experienced." Cook named the rocky headland cliffs Cape Foulweather.

For seven days and nights, Ledyard and the others endured high seas, contrary winds, hail, sleet, and snow as the ships struggled blindly along the dangerous coast in search of a safe harbor. "We can neither forward our Matters by tracing the Coast, nor have the Satisfaction of getting into a Harbour to take a look at the country," Clerke complained on March 14, 1778. Four days later, the "heavy, dull disagreeable" weather hadn't improved. In darkness and battering gales they missed the fifteen-mile-wide opening now known as Juan de Fuca Strait, which early Spanish mapmakers boasted was the

Ledyard peered eagerly through fog, rain, and wind to catch his first glimpse of the northwest coast of North America. These sketches were made by William Bligh.

entrance into the Northwest Passage. Here they could have found safe harbor on the other side of what is now called Vancouver Island.

Meanwhile, cold, wet, thirsty, and hungry, Ledyard and the *Resolution* crew staggered about their duties. Life aboard ship became a kind of nightmare. Only the hardy cockroaches, which had infested the ship in New Zealand, seemed unaffected by the miserable conditions. The insects crawled by the thousands through the dwindling food supplies, riddling anything left out into honeycomb shapes. They destroyed Anderson's precious stuffed birds and nibbled the ink from his specimen labels. The sound of the moaning wind and the clattering of thousands of crawling cockroaches and scampering rats tortured the men trying to sleep below deck. The crew tried smoking out the cockroaches and rats. Unfortunately, nothing worked.

Not until March 29 did the fierce gale weaken enough so that they could see the country, "full of high Mountains whose summits were covered with snow," Cook wrote. The fragrant hillsides covered with hemlock, cedars, and spruce sloped gently toward the water. Cook named it Hope Bay.

A lucky breeze blew the two ships into an inlet in the early evening. The breeze died, and the ships were towed farther into the sound with boats rowed by the marines and other crew members. Large flocks of noisy birds wheeled overhead. They had arrived in what Cook named King George's Sound (later renamed Nootka Sound, on Vancouver Island) not a moment too soon. Low on water, wood, and food supplies, both ships were also in dire need of repairs.

"It was [a] matter of doubt with many of us," Ledyard wrote, "whether we should find any inhabitants here, but we had scarcely entered the inlet before we saw that hardy, that intriped, that glorious creature man approaching us from the shore."

Several dozen massive, forty-foot-long dugout canoes cruised closer. Each canoe had a raised head and stern that reminded some of the crew of Viking ships. The canoes were not decorated with paint or carving.

The unarmed Nootka Indians carried lightweight paddles shaped at one end like large leaves. As they approached, a few of the men stood up and shouted and "made many strange Motions, sometimes pointing to the shore & at other times speaking to us in a confused Manner," wrote *Resolution* Sur-

Critical repairs began as soon as the ships dropped anchor at Ship Cove (now known as Resolution Cove) on Bligh Island in what Cook at first called King George's Sound (now known as Nootka Sound).

geon's First Mate David Samwell, a twenty-seven-year-old Welshman with a gift of poetry. Lieutenant James King found their speech "a Violent way of talking, seemingly with vast difficulty in uttering the Harshest, & rudest words."

What happened next came as a breathtaking surprise. The Indians began to sing what seemed to be a kind of greeting. All work, all talk aboard the *Resolution* ceased in order to listen to the haunting song that was, King admitted, "by no means unpleasant to the Ear."

"This was the first fair opportunity after our arrival that I had of examining the appearance of those unknown aborigines of North America," Ledyard said. Like King, Ledyard believed that the Indians sang because they were glad to see them.

A Nootka Indian whose body was painted red and whose face was white leaped up on a board laid across a canoe. He gestured extravagantly. His hair was ornamented with large feathers that were tied with stiff sinew in such a way that they protruded in all directions like a halo. Cook offered the visitor a piece of baize, or green cloth.

The Indian was not impressed. *"Tike'mily. Tike'mily,"* he demanded. He showed through sign language that what he wanted was iron. Clearly, Cook and his crew were not the Indian's first contact with white men. Cook lowered some medals and beads. The Indian took these graciously and hurled some dried herring up into the ship in trade.

The sun began to set. A cluster of canoes lingered in the retreating light. While the Indians beat their paddles against the sides of the wooden canoes, one repeated words that the chorus picked up in call and response. A young Indian man with a soft, sopranolike voice performed a solo. The abrupt end to his song and his final, peculiar gesture surprised Ledyard and the others so much that they burst into laughter. The singer was not displeased. He repeated the song several more times.

A man of Nootka Sound

When he finally finished, Ledyard and the other marines decided that the Indians might like to hear a fife and drum performance. "These were the only people we had seen," King wrote, "that ever paid the smallest attention to those or any of our musical Instruments."

The Indians listened in rapt silence. When the tune was finished, they sang again. Next, a sailor played a French horn. The sound wailed across the bay. As the last note of the horn echoed among the trees, the concert ended. Now it was too dark to see.

Even though no one aboard the *Resolution* or the *Discovery* understood the Indians' words, the music had made a profound connection. Ledyard lingered on the deck and looked east toward the dark outline of the shore. He felt a rush of emotion. "It was the first time . . . I had been so near the shores of that continent which gave me birth from the time I at first left it; and though more than two thousand miles distant from the nearest part of New-England I felt myself plainly affected." Thinking about his birthplace, he said, "soothed a home-sick heart, and rendered me very tolerably happy."

On the other side of the continent, farther away than he could imagine, were his family and everything familiar, everything he had fled. Suddenly, he had a remarkable idea—a suitably dramatic return for himself. A heroic arrival guaranteed to impress his relatives. What if he were to cross the North American continent from this direction, west to east? What if he strode into his mother's house and announced himself?

The next morning the ships' decks and the shoreline beyond glinted with hoarfrost. In early light the Indians paddled closer. Cook sent Lieutenant James King and ship's master William Bligh with armed marines in three boats to search for a good harbor. Cook hoped to find lumber to replace the mast as well as a place to set up the tent in order to make astronomical observations. Cook told them to spot a location as far away as possible from the Indian encampment or village.

His attempt to limit contact with the Indians was hopeless. Trade had already begun in earnest. The Indians exchanged delicate, soft otter pelts as well as bear, raccoon, polecat, and wolf skins for a nail or two. The Indians sold wild onions, shellfish, live squirrels, even bright-colored hummingbirds.

A small group of sailors bought some other strange souvenirs: three human hands and several skulls. The bones made some of the crew nervous. Were these Indians cannibals? To find out for certain, Bayly, the astronomer, promised an Indian some iron and brass if he would eat the hand that he had just traded. The contemptuous Indian refused and departed angrily. He no doubt had his own misgivings about these white barbarians.

Low prices for fine furs interested Ledyard and the other sailors. Unfortunately, they did not have much to trade. As Surgeon's First Mate David Samwell explained, they had been "so lavish with our Spike nails & Hatchets among the beautiful Girls of the South Sea Islands we had but few of these Articles left." In New Albion, a piece of iron hoop just five inches long was worth as much as twelve in the South Sea Islands. One Indian was said to try and sell a five-year-old child for a spike nail. What the Indians wanted most of all were metal buttons and pieces of copper or brass. The sailors stripped their uniforms of these. They knocked pans and teakettles to pieces.

Indians eager for trade swarmed the ships. "We had the company of the natives all day," Cook wrote, "who now laid aside all manner of restraint, if they ever had any, and came on board the Ships and mixed with our people with the greatest freedom."

Ledyard studied their visitors and made an astonishing discovery. "I had no sooner beheld these Americans than I set them down for the same kind of people that inhabit the opposite side of the continent." They reminded him of the Indians from New England.

While King called the Indians "excessive filthy," Ledyard described them as "rather above the middle stature, copper-colored, and of an athletic make. They have long black hair, which they generally wear in a club on the top of the head, they fill it when dressed with oil, paint and the downe of birds. They also paint their faces with red, blue and white colours."

Always the astute observer of clothing, Ledyard noted that they wore fringed skin clothing with two other sort of garments. "The one is made of the inner rind of some sort of bark twisted and united together like the woof of our coarse cloaths, the other very strongly resembles the New-Zealand

Webber traded all his coat buttons with an enterprising Nootka Indian in exchange for permission to draw this house. In the right foreground a smaller boat arrives with crew members, including marines.

Togo, and also principally made with the hair of their dogs." They wore no shoes or trousers, in spite of the cold. What amazed Ledyard was that they traded in wampum, beads made from shells. This was the same form of money used by Iroquois on the other side of the continent.

It wasn't long before Cook complained of the Indians' "thievish tricks . . . the instant our backs were turned." On board ship the light-fingered Indians used their knives to deftly cut ropes attached to hooks of all kinds, including one used for bringing up the anchor. They worked in teams, entertaining the sailor who was supposed to guard the deck while the other Indians stripped the place of "every article of iron about them worth carrying away," Cook wrote.

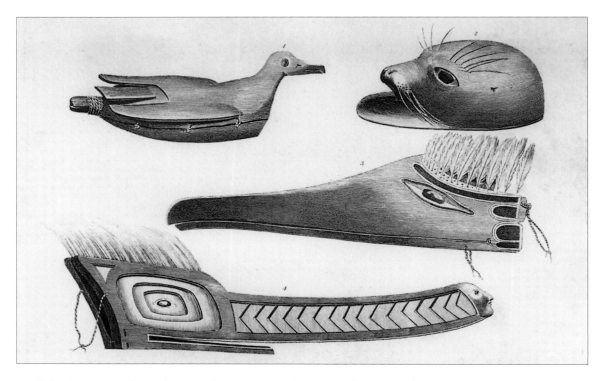

Nootka-carved wooden masks and a colorful rattle (upper left) in the shape of a bird and filled with pebbles. The rattle was used to accompany the accomplished Nootka singers, who impressed the crew with their melancholy melodies.

One boat keeper became so tired of trying to stop constant pillaging, he picked up a board and angrily threw it at the offender. He missed the Indian but damaged his canoe. Lieutenant Phillips saw the furious Indian draw his bow to shoot an arrow. Phillips fired first with a bow he'd recently traded. Fortunately, he missed. The Indian was so startled, he loaded his own weapon into his canoe and quickly paddled away.

Most visits were peaceful. Indians circled around the ships in their canoes. Some wore ornate painted masks of animals and human faces. Others rattled instruments in the shape of birds. They acted out fantastic entertainments and dramas. And always there was singing. Every evening as part of a farewell, the larger canoes saluted the ships by circling and giving three "halloos" at their departure.

First Lieutenant Burney, more musical than anyone, was struck with the beauty of the Nootka Indian song and chanting. "They paddled in excellent time," he noted, "the foremost man every 3d or 4th Stroke making flourishes with his paddle. The halloo is a single note in which they all join in, selling it out in the middle and letting the Sound die away. In a Calm with the hills around us, it had an effect infinitely superior to what might be imagined from any thing so simple."

The Indians reminded Ledyard of the "Ben Occums," as he called the remaining Connecticut and New Hampshire tribes back home. He found both groups "bold and ferocious, sly and reserved, not easily provoked but revengeful." The fearless, independent spirit of the Indians made an impression on the sailors and on Cook as well.

The captain soon discovered that the Indians had a strong sense of private property. "They intimated to us that the country all round further that we could see was theirs," Ledyard wrote. For wood and water, however, the Indians charged nothing. One day Cook approached an Indian through sign language to make certain that wood and water were free.

Perhaps Cook's persistent tone of voice or his overbearing manner irked the Indian. For whatever reason, the Indian was clearly insulted. He took Cook by the arm and vigorously thrust him away as if to tell him to mind his own business.

Cook's expression betrayed shock. Then he turned to Ledyard and a few other crew members and said with a kind of grudging admiration, "This is an American indeed!"

Chapter 9

"Not Without Hopes of the Dear Passage"

From Nootka Sound to Prince William Sound
April–May 1778

During the next three weeks, the crew caulked the sides of the badly leaking ships and repaired rotten rigging. They chopped and loaded wood, filled water casks, and brewed spruce beer. They were in a race with time. Only twelve weeks remained in the season and they still had 1,600 miles to travel. What kind of rugged ice and weather would they experience to the north?

While the foremast was pulled out and hauled ashore for repairs, Cook joined a party to go into the woods to locate and cut down a proper tree to make into the new mizzenmast. He drove the men hard, always keeping an eye on the wind and weather.

Discovery crew members were particularly adept at smuggling Indian women on board. The first thing they did was to perform what they described as "purification ceremonies," a bath with warm water and soap in a tub on deck. "This ceremony appeared very strange to the Girls," Samwell wrote, "who in order to render themselves agreeable to us had taken particular pains to daub their Hair and faces well with red oaker which to their great astonishment we took as much pains to wash off."

Pewter plate became the medium of exchange to pay for a woman's company. Dinnerware quickly vanished. Nothing would have been left for eating meals if Watman had not stowed away coconut shells in Hawaii for dishes. His foresight came from his experience on the earlier voyage.

Ledyard enjoyed going ashore and visiting with the Indians as much as he could. "Like all uncivilized men they are hospitable," he said. As a guard on an expedition into one of the villages, he noted how the Indians graciously offered the white visitors whale blubber, dried herring, and mussels to eat. The village consisted of six hundred people who lived in houses made of wooden planks. Several families shared one house.

A few of the Indians wore copper bracelets and earrings. Ledyard also noticed three or four rough-wrought knives with coarse wooden shafts that were made in a European fashion. Where had these come from? Since he couldn't speak the language, Ledyard was never able to find out. He wondered if these were trade items that had come all the way from Hudson Bay. "It seems intirely conclusive to suppose no part of America is without some sort of commercial intercourse," Ledyard wrote. His vision of transcontinental trade was far ahead of its time.

Accompanying Cook on short missions away from the humdrum rou-

Woman of Nootka Sound in woven rain hat. Surgeon's First Mate David Samwell described Nootka women as "very modest and timid."

tine aboard the *Resolution* sometimes provided a fleeting look that showed a different side of their captain. Trevenen, the youngest midshipman, who rowed thirty miles on an expedition to study botany, recalled that Cook "would sometimes relax from his almost constant severity of disposition, & condescend now and then to converse familiarly with us. But it was only for the time, as soon as we entered the ships, he became again the despot." Glimpses of the relaxed Cook would become rarer and rarer, however.

On April 23 Ledyard heard yet another story of their captain's temper. While loading the astronomer's instruments on board the ship to get ready to leave, an Indian stole a small piece of iron and jumped into his canoe. Cook

Interior of a Nootka house shared by several families. Dried fish hang from the ceiling.

flew into a rage. He grabbed a musket loaded with small shot, fired into the canoe, and wounded three or four men in their backs. The incident created such an angry stir among the other Indians, they refused to engage in any more trade that day. After so much thievery, why did this minor act cause Cook to react with musket fire?

By the time the expedition was ready to leave, on April 26, the weather cleared. In the distance, snow still dusted the hills. That afternoon they entered the open sea again, and were immediately hit by strong gales and squally weather. It was so rainy and foggy that Ledyard and the others on board the *Resolution* could not see the length of the ship.

The next day the ships were battered by what Cook called "a perfect hurricane." It was too dangerous to run any longer before the wind. At that exact moment, the *Resolution* sprang a leak "of an alarming nature," Ledyard wrote. Water rushed in near the ship's stern. Ledyard and the others below sloshed up to their knees in icy seawater. Unlashed casks, heavy enough to crush a man, bobbed dangerously back and forth below deck.

By evening the wind abated some of its fury but picked up again by nightfall. The *Resolution* lost sight of the *Discovery*. Ledyard and the rest of the crew wondered if during the night they might be driven ashore and crash upon the rocks.

The crew manned the pumps. There was no time and no opportunity to make repairs as long as the storm raged. Ledyard found out later that a hole had been eaten through the bottom of the ship "as far as the sheathing" by rats. The strain of the storm caused the sheathing to give way. Cook's luck held, however. The hole was stopped up by some "old shakings of yarn and oakum," Ledyard said, "that by some accident was washed into it."

Two days went by before the two ships made contact again. In the meantime it soon became clear that Cook's only guide was a fraud. Touted as the most up-to-date, "very accurate Little map . . . of the new discovered Northern Archipelago," Jacob Von Stählin's chart was published in 1774 in Germany to much acclaim. Von Stählin had based his imaginative findings on a Russian naval officer's explorations. The map featured a large shattered island called "Alaschka." A hopeful-looking ice-free passage was shown snaking between

Alaschka and the bulging fist labeled North America Great Continent. This route arched over an unfrozen sea stretching across the top of North America and leading back to the Atlantic.

Between bouts of bad and good weather, the crews of the *Resolution* and *Discovery* cruised north along the North American coast, always keeping a lookout for a bay or wide river leading to Von Stählin's passageway. But the farther they traveled, the more they became aware that the landmass of the Great Continent arched southward and westward—not at all what the map had revealed. The coast, Cook wrote, "seemed to be much broken, forming bays and harbours every two or three leagues or else appearences very much deceived us." It was clear they were in completely uncharted territory.

Dauntless, Cook pushed north. He was determined to follow his orders to begin exploration "as far as the latitude of 65 degrees, but taking care not to lose any time in exploring rivers or inlets." His instructions ordered him to start probing the coast for the passage no later than June. He was already a year behind schedule and the present season was quickly disappearing.

To Ledyard and the others aboard the *Resolution*, the unpromising landscape and their captain's impatience to hurry north fostered a growing sense of confusion and worry. When would they stop to fix the leaking ship? How much farther before they reached snow-shrouded land where repairs would be difficult and supplies scarce? With each passing mile, their dreams of discovering a Northwest Passage began to shrivel.

On May 7, the weather cleared up enough for a boat to be lowered for the carpenters to try and keep the leak from growing larger. Finally, on May 12, as they stood along the coast, they spied the first opening they'd seen in the land since they left St. George's Sound. "Hopes of a passage were somewhat revived," Samwell confided.

The officers passed Von Stählin's map back and forth among themselves. Ledyard peered eagerly toward shore. "We are kept in a constant suspense," said King. "Every new point of land rising to the Soward damps our hopes till they are again reviv'd by some fresh openings to the Noward."

When the ships reached what is now called the Gulf of Alaska, they entered an inlet and headed north. Would this show them the way to the pas-

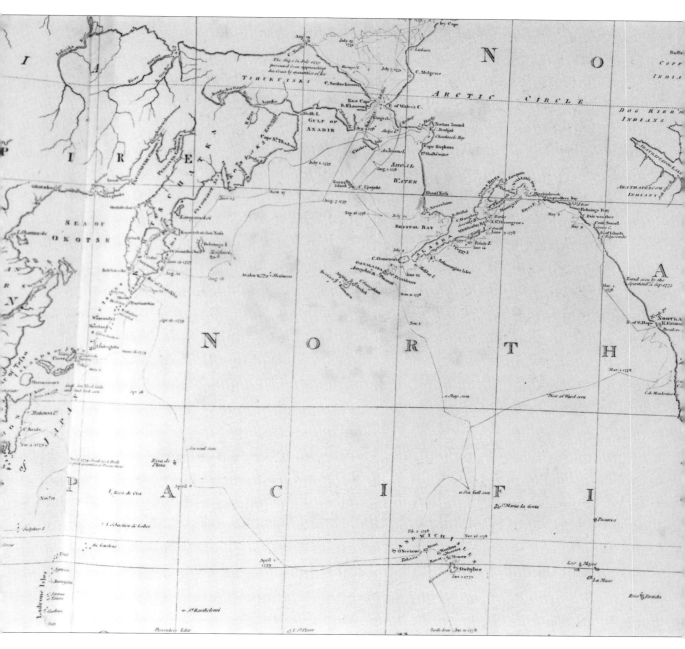

The search for the Northwest Passage, which took the ships from Hawaii, up the coast of North America, to Siberia, and back again.

sage? Gore in his characteristically positive tone named this southwestern point of Hinchinbrook Island Cape Hold-With-Hope.

Once the fog cleared, Ledyard saw that the harbor stretched wide and promising. Beyond lay desolate, windswept land shrouded in snow. There was not a sign of smoke from a cooking fire or any other human habitation.

Perhaps infected by Gore's enthusiasm, Ledyard remained cautiously hopeful. "Though the weather was bad [we] pursued our course up the inlet not without hopes of the dear Passage, which was now the only theme."

Finally, Cook ordered the ships to anchor. The men dropped nets into the water. Unfortunately, since they were torn, no fish were caught. Cook ordered Lieutenant Gore ashore with two boats to hunt for waterfowl and any other fresh game. Gore seemed delighted. Ledyard was undoubtedly even more pleased, since he was invited along. As usual, he looked for any opportunity to distinguish himself from the other Jack Tars.

For once the weather cooperated. Ledyard felt a sense of relief to be away from the crowded, leaking ship. He and several other marines rowed the oars of the pinnace across the frigid bay. Flocks of wary ducks and snow geese filled the air with warning cries.

When they reached the opposite shore, they moored the small boat, disembarked, and hunted on unsteady sea legs. Soon it was time to return. "We had some success," Ledyard said, "and being engaged in our sports, and not suspecting the country from its unhospitable appearance to be inhabited were surprized when we saw several large boats full of Indians already close upon us from behind a small island."

Twenty Indians paddled closer in two canoes. What should Ledyard and the others do? They were clearly outnumbered. The *Resolution* was moored too far away to hear their shouts for help. Nervously, they loaded the only four guns they had among them. As highest officer, it was Gore's call. What would he order them to do? Kill a few Indians or hope for the best and simply use a display of force?

Gore hesitated. Finally, he spoke. Let the Indians come within musket range. Then row as fast as you can toward the ships, he told the men. It was a gamble. The Indians in the canoes waved their spears and shouted hello. They made signs that they only wanted to trade. "We returned them for answer as well as we could to follow us, and we would trade," Ledyard said.

As soon as the men on board the *Resolution* saw the pinnace hurrying back

Native people arrived in canoes as soon as the ships harbored in Snug Corner Bay, Prince William's Sound, to make repairs on the damaged Resolution.

followed closely by two large canoes filled with Indians, they assumed a chase was in progress. Immediately, boats packed with armed marines were lowered from the *Resolution* and the *Discovery*. Gore barked to the marines to retreat peacefully.

The canoes circled warily around the ships. The Indians, in fur clothing, gestured and called to the sailors. "They all shouted & sung something in the Manner of the Inhabitants of St. George's Sound," noted Samwell.

Cook gestured in sign language for the Indians to come closer. He held up pieces of wire and a glass bowl to entice them. The Indians paddled within throwing distance. One hurled a dart on deck. Cook wrapped a piece of copper wire around the dart and tossed it back. Immediately, the satisfied Indian took the wire and placed it around his arm as a bracelet. Another piece of wood was thrown down to the canoe with some "brass wire & other trifles."

The canoes lingered about two hours. Never once did any of the Indians venture on board the ships. Only one Indian came close enough to the *Discovery* to exchange his waterfowl-skin frock for a glass bowl. As soon as the trade was made, both canoes headed for shore, "paddling & singing with all the Jollity imaginable," *Discovery* Captain Clerke wrote. "We either found these good folks on one of their Jubilee Days, or they are a very happy Race."

Ledyard had reason to feel pleased as well. He had followed orders and behaved bravely. In a tight spot, no shots were fired. Gore, he hoped, would take note of him now.

The next morning the ships left the harbor and headed immediately into what Clerke called "confounded, Foggy weather." It was nearly impossible to see the shoreline. Where could they find a snug place to repair the ship's damaged bottom? Not until May 15 was a suitable, protected harbor located. The crew tipped the *Resolution* over to one side to begin patching the hole.

Almost immediately, Indians in skin canoes and kayaks arrived. They eagerly heaped great piles of skins on shore to trade for blue and green and clear beads. A few climbed aboard the *Discovery* and stole anything within reach. The men drew cutlasses and chased them off the ship. While the *Resolution* was tipped, Indians crept close enough to smash every scuttle, the covered hatchways on the hull. Cook flew into a fit of anger. More delays!

Gore refused to worry about their timetable. Instead he gave optimistic names to surrounding snow-clad mountains and nearby landmarks: Mount Welcome, Land of Good Prospect.

Not only the land but the people looked different from any others they had encountered before. Ledyard called the inhabitants of what is now Prince William Sound "Esquimaux." Their sealskin clothing and boots and bearskin mittens and shoes and one-person skin kayaks with double-headed paddles were unique. "The Faces of many of these Indians are much like the Chinese," Samwell wrote.

Most intriguing of all were the Indians' favorite trade items. Where had they first encountered European-made blue and green beads? Had these come from Hudson Bay? On May 17, after failed attempts to find out anything through sign language from the Indians about any surrounding straits—would they lead north to some hidden passage?—Cook ordered the ships to weigh anchors and sail out of the sound back to the open sea. Ten precious days had passed, and they still seemed no closer to finding the Northwest Passage.

Man of Prince William Sound displayed the ornamented slit under lip. Sky blue glass beads were the preferred trade item for decorating hats and creating facial ornaments.

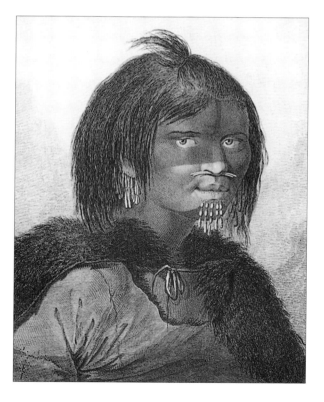

A woman of Prince William Sound

Chapter 10

"AS COMPACT AS A WALL"

From Prince William Sound to the Bering Strait
May–August 1778

The coast of what is now called Alaska's Kenai Peninsula appeared broken and splintered in a maze of little islands. The ships followed the southwest curve of the peninsula to see where it might lead. The names given the uncharted capes reflected the rise and fall of anticipation: Cape Lost Hope and Hope's Return. The ships zigzagged around headlands and in and out of the mouths of what they hoped were rivers—always to be disappointed. Time was running out.

Ledyard's spirits remained high. "Found ourselves in what we conjectured to be a vast river," Ledyard wrote on May 30, 1778, when they entered what is now called Cook Inlet. "Having a strong southerly current—sounded 40 fathoms. This gave us hopes again of a Passage." The current was thick and muddy and followed a riverbed of yellow clay. The surrounding land was peppered with striking snow-covered mountains and rushing streams.

A few days later they entered a large bay. "Found the water brakish," Ledyard wrote. The saltiness of the water gave the men hope. Did it connect with an ice-free sea to the north?

The atmosphere on board was becoming steadily strained. Debate raged between Cook, who seemed uncharacteristically indecisive, and Gore, optimistic as ever. According to Admiralty orders, they were to arrive at latitude

65 degrees north, the Arctic Circle, by June. It was already the end of May. Gore insisted that following the river was worth a try. Prickly Bligh announced that this would be a waste of time, nothing more. Still, Cook wavered.

Indians appeared in canoes with red and blue beads hanging as decorations from their pierced noses and lips. They paddled kayaks and wore fur jackets made from the skins of white rabbits. Again, the crew was frustrated in not being able to communicate. If Cook and the others could only speak to these people, wouldn't they find the information they needed? Where did the river empty?

After eleven days of exploration, the river branched and seemed to go nowhere. The wild goose chase led them back to latitude 58 degrees north. Cook ordered the ships south and west again. It was a disappointing turn of events. He named the waterway River Turnagain.

On June 6, before their departure, Cook complained privately in his journal. He had been "induced very much against my own opinion and judgment, to pursue the Course I did, as it was the opinion of some of the Officers that we should certainly find passage to the North."

Cook went on shore briefly and looked out over the disappointing flat land that would one day be the site of Anchorage, Alaska. In the distance rose a daunting wall of snowy mountains. The men hoisted a British flag, claimed the land for the king, then drank a bumper of porter, a dark brown beer.

They had lost sixteen days. To make matters even worse, the wind was against them as they struggled downriver to return to the sea. The *Resolution* ran aground on a muddy shoal. Cook was furious. Then the *Discovery* narrowly missed becoming stuck as well.

It took nearly a week to creep back to the open sea. As soon as they did, fog swallowed them. "We cleared the inlet which we called Hinchinbroke-Sound," Ledyard wrote, "the navigation of which had been very fatiguing."

Another week of rain and fog passed. On June 18 they were even farther south than they had expected—latitude 55 degrees north. From the *Discovery* suddenly came the report of three guns. This startled Ledyard and everyone else aboard the *Resolution*. What was wrong?

A boat was sent for pale, thin Clerke, who came aboard the *Resolution* to talk with Cook. He told the captain that several natives had brought to his ship a box containing a piece of paper with strange, backward-looking letters. Was it some kind of message in Russian? The only thing anyone could decipher was "1778" and "1776." Some of Cook's officers believed it might be from shipwrecked Russian sailors begging for rescue.

Nonsense, said Cook.

When the rest of the crew heard of Cook's refusal to investigate further, they felt outraged. A sailor, according to the unwritten rule, would do anything to help a fellow tar in distress. This was their first note from the outside world since leaving Table Bay, in Africa. Yet Cook decided the message wasn't worth their time.

Probably from a Russian merchant, he said. Proceed forward.

Some of the men grumbled.

The ships groped along the Kenai Peninsula as the weather kept up a round of fog and rain. Cook missed the ten-mile-wide Unimak passage through the Aleutian Islands. It was as if he were running blind now—uncertain of what deadly islands or rocks might lie ahead.

Throwing caution to the wind on June 26, Cook decided to head west through the islands like a thread through a needle. The suffocating fog was so thick, no one could see a hundred yards ahead as they passed through what is now called Unalga Pass, between Unalga and Unalaska Islands.

"About 7 in the evening we saw distant land bearing nearly south," Ledyard wrote. "By 10 o'clock we had a thick fog; fired signal guns to the Discovery and burnt false fires. At 3 o'clock in the morning heard the noise of a surf, sounded 24 fathoms. The noise of the surf encreasing we were alarmed; fired a signal of distress and came to anchor with the Discovery just under our lee."

They had stopped in the nick of time, although they did not know this until the fog finally lifted. They were only a few hundred yards from smashing into rocks that surrounded them on deadly islands on three sides. "We found ourselves embayed with rocks, reefs, and an island, all within two cables length. We were not only amazed to find ourselves in such a frightful situation, but were still more astonished to conceive how we got there."

It seemed like a miracle.

Some pointed to the old Cook luck again. Others were aghast. "Tho we were lying very safe, yet, we could not help being struck with horror at the sight of the dangers we had escaped. . . . Six minutes longer we should have run on shore," said Midshipman George Gilbert.

They had inadvertently harbored at Unalaska Island; Cook named it Providence. They stayed for two days to collect what they could find of wood, water, and fish—all in short supply. Smaller boats were sent out to sound the depths and try to chart a plan for their retreat.

Throughout their stay, they were visited by Indians bearing trade items such as furs, salmon, and other dried fish. Ledyard watched from the deck with the other sailors as the Indians paddled quickly toward them. "They did not hesitate to come near enough to converse and traffic, but would not come on board of us," wrote Ledyard. They seemed oddly polite, almost groveling. They bowed and took off their hats. They even used tobacco and snuff— much to some of the sailors' delight. (They had none left themselves.) Clearly, these Indians were familiar with Europeans.

A man of Unalaska Island, one of the most easterly of the Aleutian Islands

"They were tall, well made, wild fierce looking people in skin-canoes," Ledyard wrote of their visitors. They reminded him of the people from St. George's Sound. It was clear there was some kind of Russian influence here, but no one could tell exactly what.

Volcanoes erupted in the distance "emitting smoke but no fire," Cook noted. Finally, on the morning of June 28, with a light breeze from the south, the ships slowly made their way north through the shallow, narrow passage. Once in the Bering Sea, they met with contrary winds and thick fogs. They lingered in Samgunuda Harbor (English Bay) near the northern coast of Unalaska Island among friendly natives, who provided them with fish in exchange for a few leaves of tobacco.

Not until July 2 were the ships able to backtrack east, following the curve of the Aleutian Islands. The route followed the land like a finger tracing the profile of a face: up the lips, around the nose, and then back again toward the forehead. Without reliable charts, the ships tried to stay close to the coast of what is now Alaska and push farther and farther north.

The Bering Sea was an unpredictable, startling world. One minute Ledyard and the other men were surrounded by penetrating arctic light that dazzled and bounced off deep blue ocean. Another moment they encountered hulking, castle-shaped ice formations. These huge, slow-moving icebergs were topped by pointed spires covered with snow. The icebergs' centers were often deep indigo blue. Shadows outlined crevices. Waves dashed against the icebergs' bases. Every so often Ledyard and the others heard the thundering noise of ice ripping free and crashing into the water.

The most terrifying moments were when the ships were suddenly surrounded by blinding fog and sleeting rain. Once for nearly twenty-four hours the men heard the *whoosh* overhead of migrating curlews and ducks, but never once spied land or sun. The ships ran almost blind among deadly icebergs. Only when the clouds briefly parted could Cook or his officers gauge the sun's position and chart their latitude with any certainty.

July vanished. They hugged the Alaskan coast. As they crawled north, the air became colder, drier. Neither Ledyard nor anyone else on board the *Resolution* had seen Anderson in more than a month. Samwell, his assistant, did what he could to ease the dying doctor's wrenching coughs. Anderson's tuberculosis had reduced him to skin and bones. The brutal cold only increased his suffering.

On August 1, the ships edged closer to the Bering Strait, the fifty-mile-wide stretch of water separating North America from Asia. The next day the beloved doctor died.

Described by Cook as "a Sensible Young Man, an agreeable companion, well skilld in his profession," Anderson would be deeply missed. The easy-going surgeon was a rare character on board the *Resolution*. He got along with everyone, from lowly seaman to officer. Although Anderson had known from the beginning of the voyage that he was doomed, he remained steady, self-controlled, uncomplaining throughout the ordeal of his illness.

What would happen to them now that he was gone? "If we except our Commander," King said, Anderson's death was "the greatest publick loss the Voyage could have sustaind." There was no other man trained in medicine with as much experience to replace him. "His funeral ceremonies," Ledyard wrote, "were decently performed according to the custom of the sea." Anderson's body was wrapped in sacking and committed to the deep with all honors. Cook named a small island east of St. Lawrence Island in his honor.

There was little time to mourn as the ships headed north. In the distance Ledyard and the others could see beyond the Arctic Circle to the open Chukchi Sea. Cook seemed almost buoyant. Maybe this time they'd make the passage.

On August 9, they sailed past "the Western extremity of all America hitherto known," a place Cook named Cape Prince of Wales. A storm with piercing cold wind hit and drove them west to Siberia.

A small group went ashore in a pinnace. The men stepped on Asian soil for the first time. Ledyard and the others landed in two cutters and stood guard on shore while Cook approached a gathering of the Mongoloid Chukchi, who seemed terrified. The women grabbed their children and ran into the hills. Approximately fifty men brandished spears and bows and made menacing motions. Cook moved fearlessly among them, unarmed. From his pockets he distributed some trinkets and a bit of tobacco. In return they gave him some walrus teeth.

What Ledyard witnessed at that moment was the old Cook, the peaceful, fearless Cook of the first two voyages. The one who had a gift for cultivating native friendship.

When the rest of the men came ashore, they enjoyed trade with the Chukchi, who seemed familiar with tobacco and snuff. The natives danced to drums and showed Ledyard and the other men their domelike homes made from whale bones and wood covered with walrus skin. The sailors traded iron and beads for small pieces of ivory carved with the images of dogs and reindeer pulling sleds.

Their visit was enjoyable but brief. For once the sun shone. Flies buzzed in the warmth. The ground sprouted with hardy green grass and moss. Ledyard and the other sailors were filled with hope that perhaps the elusive Passage might be ice-free and within their reach. Maybe all their hard work and sacrifice had been worth it.

The two ships left Siberia and headed east again on August 11. As soon as they were at sea, the clear, sunny skies vanished. "The weather," Ledyard wrote, "of a sudden became piercing cold." Frozen rigging bloodied their hands, which were numb from frostbite. Running ropes froze in the blocks. The sails became as stiff as sheets of iron. The deck turned slick with ice.

Undaunted, Cook pushed north through gales and rain. Only now and again could they see the coast. It appeared snow-free. That was encouraging, wasn't it? On August 15, they had pushed as far north in latitude as 68 degrees. The wind blew hard and the sea buffeted them with "rowling Billows," Clerke wrote. Exhausted flocks of birds no bigger than sparrows appeared out of the fog and alighted on the ship. The next morning they were found in dead feathered heaps on deck. To superstitious sailors, this did not bode well.

On the morning of August 17, they reached the latitude 70 degrees north. Just before noon they saw the deadly glimmer—a warning called "the blink." It meant only one thing: ice. At one o'clock in the afternoon, Ledyard spied miles and miles of great white floes of ice, pieces of shattered icebergs, large flat shards, and other sections nearly twenty feet tall. "We saw ice a-head,

The ships dropped anchor on Asian (now Siberian) shore in St. Lawrence Bay, where they discovered a Chuckchi village. When they arrived, the Chuckchi fled in terror, mistaking Cook and his men for Russian fur traders.

broken, detached, low," Ledyard wrote. Field ice, as it is called, is more deadly than the largest iceberg. The ships could not detect this kind of ice at night.

The *Resolution* and *Discovery* snaked slowly between jagged chunks one hundred feet across that could have easily savaged their fragile bows. The men stood in tireless watch to help direct each ship's course.

"Another island!"

"Ice ahead!"

"Keep her off a little!"

"Steady!"

Carefully, they managed to dodge the biggest ice floes. The highest latitude they would reach would be on August 18: 70 degrees 44 minutes north. The ice eventually formed a kind of twelve-foot-tall barrier, "as compact as a wall," Cook wrote. Beyond they saw ice as tall as jagged mountains.

There was no way around.

With every passing moment, the situation for the ships became more crit-

The Resolution *beating through the ice, with the* Discovery *in the distance.*
Aquatint by John Webber.

ical. They were walled in on one side by shoals and on the other by ice. If they remained much longer between the ice and the land, they would be forced ashore. Cook made the signal for the *Discovery* to tack at the same time the *Resolution* made the maneuver. The wind and Cook's famous luck were with them again. They managed to turn in time and make their way out of the trap. Cook named the nearest piece of land Icy Cape.

In the distance Ledyard and the others heard the trumpeting warning of hundreds of what they called "sea horses"—male, female, and baby walruses lounging on a house-sized ice chunk. The noisy antics of the blubbery mammals with comical faces and long tusks provided a welcome distraction after their near disaster. "They are a large unweildly sluggish animal," Ledyard wrote, "weighing some of them nine hundred and some eleven hundred weight." One sailor said the walrus cries sounded like a cross between a howling dog and a bellowing ox.

Like sailors on a precarious, icy craft, the walruses had developed their own watch system—not so different from the desperate one used aboard the *Resolution* and *Discovery*. "To prevent being suprized in their sleep [the wal-

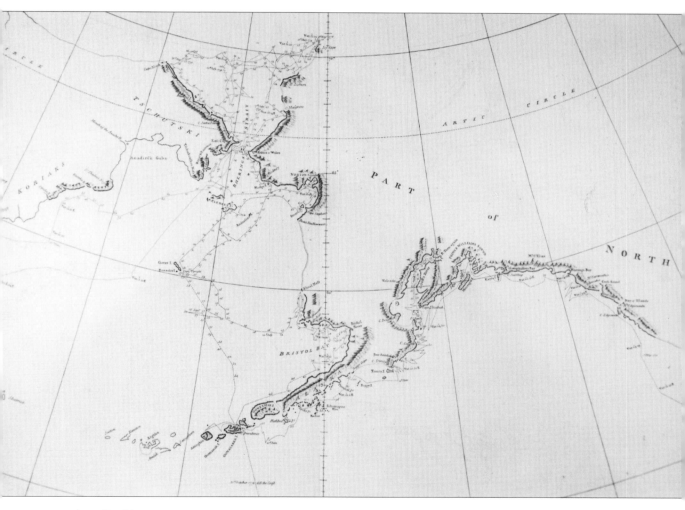

A wall of ice eventually halted the expedition's search for the Northwest Passage. The farthest north the ships reached into the Arctic Sea was 77 degrees 44 minutes north latitude.

ruses] always appoint one as a sentinall and place it in the middle to keep watch . . . an attentive eye alround," explained Gilbert. If the sentinel sensed danger, he bellowed an alarm signal. Instantly the mob plunged into the water and swam away.

In the dark and fog, walrus cries proved handy to the ships. The noise gave the sailors their notice of ice—sometimes their only warning. The walrus watch system also made hunting the animals challenging. Once the sentinel walrus sounded the warning, the others dived into the water before they could be shot and captured.

Walrus oil burned well in lamps, and strips of their tough hides proved useful in rigging. After butchering, the blubber was boiled for hours, then sliced and fried as steaks. To save what few rations were left, walrus became the main meal for breakfast, lunch, and dinner. Few besides Cook relished the rich, greasy meat.

"The people at first murmured," Ledyard wrote, "and at last eat it through mere vexation; and trying to see who would eat most in order to consume it the sooner, some of the people rather overdid the matter, which produceing some laughable circumstances. The tars swore they would eat it or any thing else that Cook did, for they were certain that nothing would kill him."

What Ledyard did not reveal was how close the men on the *Resolution* came to mutiny over having their regular rations cut. For months the hungry men had had nothing but scant servings of salt pork. Many found that walrus made them sick. Those who refused to eat the newfangled rations became too weak to work.

"You damn't mutinous scoundrels who will not face novelty!" Cook shouted at them.

At last Cook gave way to the complaining. "The discontents rose to such complaints & murmurings that he restored the salt meat," wrote Midshipman Trevenen.

This would not be the last of complaints and murmurings.

For the next ten days, the ships crisscrossed the Chukchi Sea. Unknown to Ledyard or the rest of the men, Cook had announced to his officers that they would try to reach Europe via the arctic western route. He believed he could head west over the top of Asia to reach Europe. This plan appalled King, Gore, and Bligh, who proclaimed the idea crazy. Look at the advancing ice pack, they said. The ships would never make it.

"Those are my instructions," Cook repeated angrily.

Through the night Ledyard and the others were kept awake by the sound of booming ice as the waves collided ice floes together—a noise that sounded like a heavy waterfall.

The air was raw, sharp, and cold. Cook pushed the ships past ice piled in fantastic jumbles and wild shapes—some clear, some white, some gray-green. There seemed no way to go around the floes. Cook studied the icebergs like a scientist.

The theory of the day was that only fresh water could freeze. Any ice dis-

Bellowing walruses were hunted by the crew in smaller boats. Blubber became the main ration, and nearly caused a mutiny.

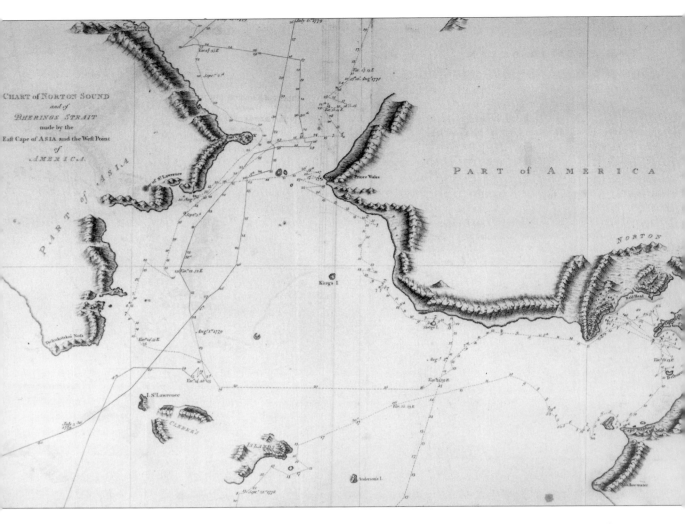

Chart of Norton Sound and the Bering Strait reveals how relentless Cook was in probing every possible opening that might lead to the fabled Northwest Passage.

covered this far to the north, it was believed, came from a distant frozen river or from snowfall. Cook gazed at the enormous icebergs, which were largely underwater. As the ice floes ground and crashed against one another, he tried to make sense of what he saw based on what he had been told. He decided there must be some kind of "endless accumulation" of the snow during many seasons. Such reasoning helped him remain hopeful that somewhere, somehow, there must be an ocean path over the top of the continent that would remain ice-free.

Meanwhile, Ledyard and the others knew that the season was growing late. Those who had been with Cook on expeditions to the Antarctic had experienced the terrifying dangers firsthand. The longer they remained among the ever-changing ice, the more likely they'd never escape alive.

The crews' prospects looked dim. They had drunk the last of the spruce beer. Their food supplies were shrinking, and they had no idea where they could be replenished. The ships themselves were in bad need of repair. Without any special sheathing, the fragile *Resolution* and *Discovery* would be ground to splinters from being pounded by wind against compressing packs of ice.

On the morning of August 29, with fog fast approaching and the beginning of another heavy snow, Ledyard heard the news. Cook announced to the ship's company that they would leave the ice as quickly as they could. They would try again next year, Cook promised.

The men cheered when they heard their commander's decision to retreat. King wrote triumphantly about "the general joy that this news gave."

Cook, of course, tried to appear indefatigable and unswerving even in the face of defeat. But as the ships began their journey south, Ledyard and the others could see what kind of strain the voyage had had on their haggard, nearly fifty-year-old commander. For six months, they had faced almost constant danger from blinding, cold weather, equipment failure, and unknown landforms.

Later on August 29, the barren Russian coast appeared for an instant and then was hidden by fog. Heavy snow fell. Water buckets froze hard on deck. For five days they could not see the shore as they made their way southeast along the Siberian arctic coast. The sun finally shone again just when they reached the middle of the Bering Strait. "Had the pleasure," Ledyard wrote, "to see both continents at once."

Chapter 11

A Chance for Greatness

From the Bering Strait to Unalaska
August–September 1778

Not until September 6, 1778, did the crews of the *Resolution* and *Discovery* see the coast of America again. Three days later the ships steered toward present-day Nome, Alaska, and into a well-wooded, large bay that Cook named Norton Sound for one of his patrons, Sir Fletcher Norton. The plan was to find a suitable place to anchor and find drinking water, fuel, and, hopefully, fresh food. They crossed the bay, taking soundings to measure the water's depth. When they reached the depth of only three and a half fathoms, very shallow water at one end of the sound, the wind suddenly blasted them toward land. Waves heaved and slapped against the shore.

"All hands!"

Ledyard and the rest of the men on board had to act quickly under Cook's expert direction to avoid disaster. All night long they tacked back and forth to get to the safety of deeper water. This was exhausting, nerve-wracking work. The ships were in danger of crashing into each other or running aground. Not until daybreak did they make six fathoms.

Some of the officers were distressed that their careless captain once again had gotten them into such a disastrous situation. "I doubt strongly whether any other Man in the world would have ventured so far he had already done; & indeed whether it was not highly imprudent," Trevenen said.

They dropped anchor on September 11 in Norton Sound behind a peninsula. Ledyard and the others were greatly relieved. They were soon visited by Indians. A man in a small canoe appeared and traded with Cook a fox-skin dress for a knife and some beads. As soon as he paddled away, another man arrived with dried salmon. "We were visited by some of the natives while here, and purchased an agreeable supply of good fish," said Ledyard. He reported "exercises on shore" that seemed to refresh everybody "who from long confinement, hard duty, scanty and almost any fare had become pale, languid and poor."

With the arrival of autumn, the sky darkened with enormous migrating flocks of ducks and geese. The bushes were heavy with berries. While Gore, Ledyard, and a party of marines went off in boats in search of firewood, they also kept a lookout for sweet, ripe raspberries, huckleberries, and red and black currants. The fresh food and physical exercise had amazing results. Ledyard claimed that he and the other sailors were "transformed into new beings almost, and were literally grown fat, plump and rosy."

They traded four rusty knives made from "old iron hoop" for nearly four hundred pounds of fine fresh fish from a family of Indians dressed in deerskin who visited them the next day. There was plenty of driftwood for fuel and an abundance of fresh water. They even found spruce trees to use to brew beer.

It wasn't long before battalions of canoes arrived with furs and salmon to trade. On September 16, their visitors provided singing entertainment, "very agreeable Musick," according to Clerke. One man beat upon a drum while another "made a thousand antic motions with his hands and body."

Perhaps it was the unseasonably mild weather, the hospitable treatment by the Indians, or the abundance of trade that reminded Cook of another place, another people. Whatever the reason, he suddenly changed his mind. Instead of wintering in Kamchatka, eastern Siberia, as he had first told his officers, they would instead spend the season farther south, in the Sandwich Islands, "where I could procure refreshments for the people and a small supply of Provisions."

As Cook explained in his journal, he didn't think Siberia would be the place "where I could procure either the one or the other for so large a number of men." And, he added, he didn't like the idea of having his men idle for six or seven months—a contradictory notion since his men had been idle for months in the Society Islands.

Once the rumor circulated that the ships were going back to paradise, the men instantly revived.

The plan was to head to a good harbor along the American coast and restock water supplies among the friendly natives of Unalaska, one of the Aleutian Islands, before making the five-week passage to the Sandwich Islands. If worse came to worse and the two ships were separated, they'd meet at Samgunuda Harbor, the name given the Unalaska bay where they had previously sought shelter.

Once they headed out of the sound and south along the coast, snow began to fall. Fog enveloped them. There were hints of Cook's exhaustion. He passed the island he had previously named after Surgeon William Anderson and recorded it as a newly discovered place. "A gross mistake!" exclaimed *Resolution* Master William Bligh.

On September 25, the *Resolution* sprang another leak. Ledyard and the others cursed as they took turns manning the pumps and bailing water all night long in rough, heavy seas.

Finally, on October 2 at daybreak, they saw Unalaska Island again. They had called the Aleutian island Providence on their visit three months earlier. Once again they reached the island just in time.

The ships were anchored and heeled over for repairs. Carpenters went immediately to work ripping off the sheathing. They discovered that many of the seams just above the waterline had opened. When Ledyard and the others saw just what kind of deplorable shape the ships were in, they were glad not to be in the arctic. "This ended," Gilbert wrote of their 1,200 leagues in the icy north, "a very hazardous and disagreeable Season."

The nearby beach of Samgunuda became a kind of colorful, noisy marketplace. Sailors stood around smoky driftwood fires and bartered beads and nails for Indians' fresh halibut, salmon, and berries by the basketful. The fresh fish and fruit were scurvy preventives after long weeks of eating salted pork in the arctic.

The voices of Indians and sailors intermingled with the sounds of axes felling trees, hammers hammering, and anvils clanging. Trade items had been depleted to such an extreme that Cook ordered the blacksmith to go to work cutting up a spare anchor. The idea was to create as many hatchets, spikes, and nails as he could to barter with the Hawaiians.

On October 8, an Indian named Derramoushk arrived with a curious, freshly baked present for Cook. "A cake of rye-meal newly baked," Ledyard said, "with a piece of salmon in it seasoned with peper and salt." This shocked Cook. A bit of European cookery in the middle of the Alaskan wilderness? It could only be from some Russians in the neighborhood.

According to Ledyard, Derramoushk told Cook through sign language, "There are some strangers in the country, who are white, and came over the great waters in a vessel somewhat like ours."

Cook consulted with several of his officers. What should they do? Present a bottle of rum and some port to "our unknown friends," Cook suggested. Who should accompany this Derramoushk and make the delivery? Gore spoke up. He volunteered the services of Ledyard.

Cook considered Ledyard "an intelligent man" who might be able to gain some useful information. Ledyard's orders, Cook said, "if he met with any Russians, or others, to endeavour to make them understand that we were English, Friends and Allies."

When Gore told Ledyard the news about his solo excursion, Ledyard was delighted. He immediately said yes. Here at last was a chance for greatness. What better way to be recommended as a heroic volunteer than by a fellow American? He felt grateful to Gore, whom he called his "intimate friend . . . at this time and ever after."

Of course, the more Ledyard thought about his dangerous mission, the more he inflated the reasons behind his selection. The way he saw it, an armed group of marines would move too slowly. If they were cut off by Indians, the loss would be "irreparable." "A single person," Ledyard said with some satisfaction, "would entirely risk his life though he would be much more expeditious if unmolested, and if he should be killed the loss would be only one."

There was something dramatic about going alone. He liked that.

On the first night of his journey Ledyard visited an Unalaskan village of thirty earth-houses thatched with grass, similar to this one. "The whole village was out to see us," he wrote.

Cook provided Ledyard with a rare private audience—another reason that made the journey worth the risk for Ledyard. "[He] assured me that he was happy I had undertaken the rout as he was conscious I should persevere," Ledyard said happily. "After giving me some instructions . . . he wished me well."

Ledyard was to be gone a week, no more. The Indian Perpheela, a "comely young chief," would be his guide. He would take along some presents: some brandy in bottles, some bread, but no other provisions. He was to go unarmed. If he weren't back in two weeks, he would be left behind.

Ledyard knew no Russian. He could not speak a word of the Indians' language. But no matter. He was thrilled. He said farewell to his fellow sailors and left immediately with Perpheela and two of his attendants.

On the afternoon of October 8, 1778, Ledyard and his guides hiked about fifteen miles over hilly, rocky country into the interior part of the island. Ledyard trudged behind his swift guides, trying his best to keep up with them. Where were they going? He had no way to find out.

Just before nightfall, they reached a village of about thirty huts. They were surprisingly large and built into the ground. In the darkness he could not see the construction very well, but they appeared to be some kind of "slight frame erected over a square hole sunk about four feet into the ground." The frame was covered with bricks made of turf. The roof was thatched with grass.

As Ledyard was led by his polite, obliging guides to the largest hut, he was immediately swarmed by villagers. Like the other Indians, his guides had holes under their lips in which they wore small stones as ornaments. "Men, women and children crouded about me," he wrote. Nervously, he made friendly signs—the same kind he had seen Cook make on the many occasions he couldn't speak the language. "I was surprized at the behavior of the Indians. . . . They did not express that extraordinary curiosity that would be expected had they never seen a European before."

Clearly, they were accustomed to seeing white men. Ledyard admitted that he felt relieved. This meant, he believed, that "there were Europeans among them."

But where?

Ledyard looked around the house. It was filled with Indians. Not a Russian among them. He described the women as "much more tolerable than I expected to have found them." One in particular, whose name he never discovered, seemed "very busy to please me." Disregarding his orders, he gave her some of the presents he'd brought along for the Russians. What exactly the gift was, he doesn't say.

Perpheela motioned to him, indicating that this was where they would eat and spend the night. Ledyard was very hungry and tired. He was glad not to go any farther. Nothing about these people gave him the least apprehension. For dinner they ate "some dryed fish, and I had some bread and some spirits," he said. Again, he wasn't exactly following the orders. The rum and porter he'd brought along were supposed to be for the Russians.

Happily, Ledyard climbed into one of the many wooden platforms that

*A woman of Unalaska displays
facial ornaments decorated with
favorite blue beads.*

*In Unalaska Ledyard slept on a platform like those shown in this interior of a communal
home. A ladder leads to the door in the roof.*

lined the walls. He fell asleep on this fur-covered bed with the skin of a bear for a blanket.

The next day he was awakened early by impatient Perpheela. "I flung off the skins I had slept in, put on my shoes and outside vest, and arose," said Ledyard. He made good-bye gestures to his hosts and headed with his three guides on a trail that veered to the southwest.

After an hour Ledyard noticed that his feet were swollen, "which rendered it extremely painful to walk." His lameness slowed down their march through the treeless, rough country. The weather turned wet and cold. Miserable Ledyard limped up and down the rocky hills. After more than two years on a ship, he wasn't much of a hiker.

At this time of year, the light began to fade quickly by late afternoon. Three hours before sunset, they came to a large bay that looked to be about "three leagues" across.

Without much ceremony, Perpheela tossed what remained of Ledyard's Russian gifts, along with his own cargo, into a hidden sealskin canoe, jumped in, and paddled away. He motioned to Ledyard to follow the other two Indians around the bay on the trail.

Perpheela's sudden disappearance, Ledyard admitted, "gave me some uneasiness." What if the fellow were stealing his belongings? What if he meant to leave him with the other two Indians, who'd murder him? He had no choice, however, but to follow the two Indians. After about six miles of walking in the rain, all the while keeping the bay in view, they spotted a two-person skin kayak speeding closer through the growing darkness. The two Indians accompanying Ledyard started jumping in the air. They waved bushes to signal the kayakers to come closer.

The waterproof double kayak made of sealskin bumped gently into the shallow bay water. The two riders signaled to Ledyard to get in. Where? Ledyard wanted to know. How?

The Indians exchanged disgusted looks that could mean only one thing. *Stupid lame white man.*

One of the Indians grunted and hoisted himself out of the kayak. He pointed into the hole.

Inside the kayak? Ledyard couldn't believe it. He crossed his arms in defiance. How could he fit? He wouldn't do it.

The Indian pointed again.

Sheepishly, Ledyard climbed into the open hatchway, lowered himself in, and wriggled inside so that he lay on his back between the two kayakers wearing waterproof fish-gut frocks. He could not see where they were going. They could take him anywhere.

Inside the kayak was dark and smelled of putrid fish, wet fur, and muddy sealskin boots. He tried not to breathe. He tried not to think about what would happen if the kayak tipped over—as he'd often seen them do near Kamchatka. There'd be no escape. He'd drown for certain.

Ledyard traveled inside a double kayak (above), lying on his back between two paddlers.

Chapter 12

RUSSIAN HOSPITALITY

Unalaska
October 1778

The kayak moved swiftly through the water, hissing as it sliced through the waves. The double paddles dipped rhythmically in the water. Had an hour passed? Or more? Ledyard couldn't tell.

Finally, he heard the paddles drag against the water. The kayak bumped and jolted, then came to a stop. There was the sound of splashing. Someone said something. Someone answered.

Ledyard felt the kayak being lifted. Someone with a deep bass voice barked orders in a language Ledyard had not heard before. *Plunk!* The kayak was placed on the ground. Two rough hands plunged into the kayak hatchway, grabbed Ledyard, and pulled him partway up. Another pair of hands joined in the tugging and wrenching. Then another.

"I was drawn out by the shoulders," Ledyard said, undoubtedly embarrassed by his unheroic entrance. This wasn't what he'd planned. His feet were asleep. His legs felt numb. He blinked as helplessly as a newborn pup.

He stumbled onto dry ground, still unable to see anyone's faces in the darkness. The bossy strangers held on to him by his elbows and guided him toward a nearby hut that looked similar to the one he'd left that morning.

A door opened. Someone held a light. At first all that Ledyard could see was a silhouette. He turned to his right, to his left. "To my joy and suprize I discovered that the two men who held me by each arm were two Europeans, fair and comely," he said. They were the Russians, the first white strangers he'd seen since they left the Cape of Good Hope, in Africa, nearly two years earlier.

Ledyard was greeted warmly by his hosts, who spoke no English. They ushered him inside. The stuffy, warm hut was filled with many Indians, who all bowed obediently. He walked to the far end of the hut, where there was a platform covered with furs. Exhausted, wet, and cold, he took a seat.

Immediately, someone brought Ledyard a change of clothes: a blue silk shirt, pants, a fur cap, and boots. Ledyard, who loved fine clothes more than anything, put these fresh garments on "with the same chearfulness they were presented with," he wrote. Then with a sudden desire to philosophize, he added, "Hospitality is a virtue peculiar to man, and the obligation is as great to receive as to confer."

This statement at this moment of his triumph would become something of his credo in later years, when he became especially adept at being on the receiving end of almost every encounter.

For now, however, Ledyard could luxuriate in the success of his mission. He had arrived. His hosts were friendly. A table was set up and heaped with European delicacies: rye bread, snuff, tobacco—all things Ledyard had not seen in such abundance in many months. He graciously presented the Russians with his remaining rum and porter. He made a little speech that these were "presents from Commodore Cook, who was an Englishman."

The Russians didn't understand a word. It didn't matter. They quickly uncorked the spirits and drank directly from the bottles. They made toasts in Russian. Ledyard made toasts in English. Someone mentioned a name.

Suddenly, everyone took off their hats. They rose. Ledyard assumed it was probably for Empress Catherine II of Russia. Even though their empress was thousands of miles away, the Russians and their Indian servants were still clearly Her Majesty's subjects. When Ledyard had left Connecticut, the frisky colonies were beginning the struggle toward independence. The Russians' extreme reverence for authority surprised and perplexed him. But he'd never insult his hosts. He toasted Empress Catherine, too.

Then he tried through painstaking sign language to tell the Russians that they were to accompany him the next day back to the ship to visit the great and powerful Captain Cook. They nodded eagerly. He hoped they understood.

Finally, Ledyard lay down in the comfortable fur bed and went to sleep. He woke briefly to see the Russians assemble the Indians for evening prayer in the Russian Orthodox tradition. Ledyard watched sprawled in his bed, eyes half-open, as the Indians mumbled over small crucifixes. He wondered if they understood anything that the Russians had told them. Then he fell into a stupor.

Late the next morning Ledyard awoke. He felt terrible. Without ceremony, however, his hosts conducted him out of the big hut into a much smaller hut several yards away. Smoke poured from a hole in the roof. Inside the hut Ledyard could barely see through the steam a number of platforms raised three feet from the ground and covered with dry coarse grass and some small green bushes. The Russians, hale and hearty after the night's entertainment, were sitting naked on the platforms. They greeted Ledyard warmly and indicated that he was to strip and take a seat.

Gingerly, Ledyard did as he was told. An Indian tossed more logs on the fire beneath a copper cauldron of boiling water. More steam rose. The temperature in the hut became hotter. And hotter still. *Clunk!* Ledyard fainted. He fell backward on the platform.

One of the Russians threw some cold water on his face to revive him. Ledyard sat up, embarrassed. I'm fine, he lied. An obedient Indian sprinkled him with soap from one of the bushy branches. Someone else sprinkled him with water. Finally, the ceremony ended. With relief, Ledyard scuttled out of the hut.

The Russians had prepared a big breakfast of greasy whale, walrus, and smoked bear meat. The smell made Ledyard, who was still very hungover, gag. He swigged a bit of brandy to feel better. He nibbled some dried smoked salmon to please the Russians. Reluctantly, he had learned his lesson. Never again would he try to out-drink a Russian.

Early in the afternoon snow began to fall. It looked like a bad day to try to

Polar bears swam among the ice floes. In August 1779 sailors hunted and killed two, five-hundred-pound bears. The meat, they complained, tasted fishy.

make it back to the ship. So Ledyard spent the rest of the afternoon writing down a few words he'd learned in Kamchatkan and compared those with what little he knew of Iroquois speech from his months in the woods outside Dartmouth.

He went for a stroll among the huts and carefully counted the number of Russians (thirty) and the number of Kamchadales, or native Kamchatkans (seventy). It seemed as if these had all converted to the Russian religion. He also discovered an old sloop docked in a cover behind the village. Nearby was a hut containing some sails, rope, and rigging.

He tried through sign language to find out who owned the ship. The only word he could make out in his investigation was "Bering." Naturally, he assumed that this must be one of the boats belonging to the famous Danish explorer Vitus Bering, who attempted to sail from Kamchatka to America in 1741. This was a wishful flight of Ledyard's fancy.

The next day Ledyard was joined by three Russians on his route back to the *Resolution*. Rather than humiliating travel crammed inside a kayak, he would make the journey in a spacious skin boat with a dozen oars. He did not have to walk at all.

Late in the afternoon of October 10, Ledyard returned to Cook's encampment with the three Russians and their attendants. He was enormously pleased with the success of his undertaking. "Before dark I got on board [the *Resolution*] with our new acquaintance," he wrote. "The satisfaction this discovery gave Cook, and the honor that redounded to me may be easily imagined."

Cook was delighted to discover that one of the Russians understood maps and appeared to be the master of a vessel. Another in the trio had very good handwriting and an excellent head for figures. Even though they could not speak the same language, the Russians spent much time in Cook's cabin as amiable cartographers, sketching routes, calculating latitude and longitude, figuring log lines or ship speed, compass points, and wind directions. "I laid before them my Chart," Cook wrote, "and found they were strangers to every part of the America Coast except what lies opposite them."

Later it turned out that the Russians had spied the *Resolution* and *Discovery* earlier on their voyage north and had kept hidden because they believed them to be Japanese invaders.

Cook found the Russians' maps to be maddening. He wanted facts. The more he probed, the more he discovered how false and sketchy the maps he had been using really were. He was especially outraged by the map made by Von Stählin, "jumbled in . . . regular confusion, without the least regard to truth."

In spite of the Russians' somewhat sloppy cartography standards, Cook and the other sailors found them to be amazingly hospitable and friendly. On October 14, the colonial governor, Gregorioff Sin Ismyloff, arrived in a magnificent fur cape. The full-bearded governor was accompanied by many local chieftains, who were unarmed. The governor was described by Master Thomas Edgar as "a very shrewd and penetrating sort of man." Ismyloff spoke fluent Aleut and Russian. Cook spoke neither. There was no way for the two men to understand each other except through sign language.

As best he could, the proud governor used crude signs to describe how the

Russians had brutally killed or conquered the warlike local Aleutian people. The Russians had efficiently taken away the native people's weapons and made them into slavelike workers who provided sea otter skins and other furs. Any theft by a native, the governor indicated, was punished by instant death.

What about rules regarding treatment of native women? Cook asked.

The governor shook his head. Russian men were not allowed to mingle freely with Aleut women. The governor seemed barely able to conceal his contempt for the unprincipled behavior of Cook's men.

Cook took in all this information as best he could. He used the Russians' regular contacts back in St. Petersburg to send a message to the Admiralty. This report, he hoped, would arrive in London before their return.

The next three weeks on the island were spent in a round of visits back and forth between the Russian-Aleut village and the ship. The British sailors exchanged liquor for Russian-made boots. With every visit, there was the obligatory round of Russian pistol shots in the air.

Winter grew colder, snowier. It was time to leave. "We had now been nine months upon the coast of America," Ledyard wrote. "We had seen and suffered a great deal, and we had still more to see no doubt, but I believe nobody thought more to suffer."

Unfortunately, Ledyard would be proved wrong.

The luxurious pelt of the sea otter would prove to be a valuable trade item when the crew reached China.

Chapter 13

RETURN TO PARADISE

From Unalaska to Hawaii
October 1778–January 1779

On October 27, 1778, Cook's fiftieth birthday, the two ships left Unalaska and set sail straight into the teeth of a terrific storm. "We have hardly experienced 4 days worse weather in the voyage," King wrote. For a week, the winds raged. A gust hurled Clerke's personal servant, a young Scotsman named John McIntosh, down the hatchway of the *Discovery*. He was killed instantly. Three other men were hurt badly.

Neither Ledyard nor anyone else aboard the *Resolution* found out about the death or the loss of the *Discovery*'s staysail until nearly twelve hours later. The two ships were separated that long without any visual contact. Indeed it seemed as if the arctic were displaying its own harsh way of bidding them farewell.

On November 15, the weather became calm enough for Ledyard and the other men to dry the ship's sails, smoke below decks, and repair rigging. A crewman on the *Resolution* spied a dolphin—the first seen on their passage south again. The sailors welcomed this as a sign that soon they'd be back in paradise.

At daybreak on November 26, exactly a month since they left Unalaska, they spied a new Hawaiian island, which they later learned was called Maui. In the distance the island looked like an elevated saddle rising above the clouds. The exquisite green land sloped toward the shore and ended in a steep rocky coast. Stretching along the edge was the dreaded white surf that meant there'd be no good landing place. Through the telescope, they spotted the familiar sight of people and thatched houses. They knew that they would soon long to find the water and food they desperately needed.

In the month since they'd left Unalaska, the temperature had risen from 38 to 81 degrees Fahrenheit. Their feelings of happiness rose as well. Cook's first order, however, sent a ripple of disappointment among the crew. "All persons," he said, "are prohibited from trading but such as should be appoint'd by me or Captain Clerke and these only for provisions and refreshments."

The second order caused even louder grumbling. No women on board, Cook said.

A splendid double canoe arrived with an old man dressed in a bright-red-feathered hat and a robe with a long train. His name, the men discovered, was Kahekili. One of his attendants carried two iron daggers called *pahoa*, which "we supposed must have had from Ships who had touched here before us," Samwell wrote. No one could explain where the mysterious daggers came from. Their appearance, however, would prove a strange omen.

Ledyard and the others had little time to contemplate the daggers or other details of their arrival. They were overwhelmed to see more than five hundred natives in canoes swarm about the ships, singing and calling out a hysterical welcome. Among this huge mass of humanity were bold young women who made lascivious motions and demanded to come on board.

But according to Cook's new rule, all women were denied entry. Cook refused to anchor. He skirted the cluster of islands and tried to chart what he could in a clockwise direction. The only food and water supplies he purchased were those brought out to the ships by canoes.

What Ledyard and the rest of the crew did not appreciate or understand was how desperate Cook was to keep control over trade and contact with natives. Cook knew there weren't enough nails to pay for needed rations. His rule to keep native women off the ships was to prevent the crew from spreading venereal disease.

A young woman of the Sandwich (now known as Hawaiian) Islands

Samwell, now serving as the surgeon, inspected the men. The *Resolution* pay book tells the story. Sixty-six men, including Ledyard, were listed as being treated for venereal disease before August 1778. More than half were afflicted. This is far more than the highest average (20 percent) listed for Royal Navy ships at the time.

A boatload of natives with painful venereal sores came alongside the ship. They told the sad tale of how they had visited the Isle "Atowi," where they picked up the disease from Cook's brief earlier visit. The natives were given some medicine, probably mercury treatments. It saddened Cook to see the suffering caused by his own men. "The evil I meant to prevent . . . ," he wrote of venereal disease, "had already got amongst them."

Again and again, Cook reported in his journal: "made Sail and stood off-shore." Natives in swift canoes managed to clamber deftly up over the sides of the ship and crowd the deck. They danced, sang, and shouted as they sold bread-fruit, potatoes, taro root, and plantains. However, if any women came aboard, they were sent away. As soon as they were forced off, they shouted abuses.

Captain Charles Clerke
portrait in oils, made in 1776
by Sir Nathaniel Dance

Ledyard and the others became increasingly impatient. Paradise was just within their grasp. Why wouldn't Cook allow them to go on shore and enjoy themselves?

On the morning of December 1, they spotted for the first time the magnificent island of Hawaii. The island's mountains stood covered with snow. Striking waterfalls fell like silver ribbons from green cliffs. Again the natives came close. Their canoes were decorated with white streamers, which seemed to be symbols of peace. Again there was limited trade. "We made sail," Cook wrote, "and stood off."

While Bayly and several others were busy observing an eclipse of the moon on December 4, Ledyard and the others could only stare out at the beautiful starry night and gaze toward the shore with great longing.

The crew had grown accustomed to going ashore to exercise and gather greens. Now they couldn't even use this activity as an excuse to escape on an amorous adventure. There were no pleasure jaunts now. Just an endless circling in rough sea of a promising tropical land they couldn't touch.

On December 7, Cook made the abrupt decision to stop serving grog every day. He did not consult any of his officers or offer up the new rule to the men the way he had in the arctic. On alternate days, he said, the men would drink a new beer made with native sugarcane. Cook found the beer tasty and thought it might help prevent scurvy. At the same time, the sugarcane beer would help save some of the grog, which was in short supply.

When Ledyard and the others refused to drink the sugarcane beer and wrote to Cook to say why, their captain was furious. How dare they? He gathered the crew on the deck and stormed at them.

"I can help you no more," Cook raged. "Every innovation of mine—portable soup, sour kraut, all of them—have been designed by me to keep my people generally speaking free from the dreadful distemper, scurvy. I cannot help it if you choose not to drink this healthful decoction. You will be the sufferers. Had you drunk it, you would have been served grog every other day. Now the grog cask will be struck down in the hold and you can content yourselves with water. This is a very mutinous proceeding. In future you cannot expect the least indulgence from me."

Cook stomped to his cabin and slammed the door.

For Ledyard and the others, this incident was worse than the walrus blubber boycott. The more the sailors discussed the injustice against them, the bigger the incident became in their minds. How dare their captain arbitrarily take away their one pleasure? How dare he disrupt the regular, dependable routine that had gone on for the past two and a half years? In their crowded wooden world, the community they had created aboard ship, there were certain routines to be followed. Breaking the routines meant possibly unleashing violence.

It may have been Ledyard's friend John Gore, or perhaps James King, who helped cool the crew's hot tempers. How exactly they may have managed it is not known. Cook doesn't say in his journal. On December 20, grog was being served again.

In spite of shark sightings, native women swam from the canoes to the strangers' ships. While they were waved away from the *Resolution*, they were lifted "like another Venus," Samwell said, "just rising from the Waves," aboard the *Discovery*. Clerke ran a much less disciplined ship. He looked the other way when his men welcomed the ladies aboard with gifts of "bracelets" the men had created with strips of red cloth decorated with buttons ripped from their own jackets. There was even a drunken brawl reported between decks on the *Discovery* on Christmas Day. The fight was so ferocious, a terrified native jumped overboard. Clearly, the old wanton days had returned—at least for the men on the *Discovery*.

Ledyard celebrated his third Christmas in a row aboard the *Resolution* out of sight of land. For the moment, time seemed to stand still. The ships were expected to return to England in 1779, the fast approaching new year. Ledyard may have wondered if his family thought he was never coming back.

With the arrival of the new year, the weather suddenly worsened. On January 1, 1779, a gale drove in clouds and hard rain. For thirteen days off the misty coast of Hawaii, the ships lost sight of each other. Stranger still, Cook had not given Clerke a rendezvous point. How could the *Discovery* simply vanish?

In the distance, on brief occasions when the clouds broke, Ledyard and the others saw the rocky, barren volcanic coastline of the treacherous southeast coast of Hawaii. There seemed no vegetation, no fresh water. The landscape appeared as unpromising as the moon. For the past ten weeks, Ledyard and the others had watched impatiently from the moving ship as island scenery shifted—from lush jungle and now this. Neither the marines nor the sailors had stepped ashore once.

Meanwhile, their ship seemed in imminent danger of falling apart. The *Resolution*'s shabby rigging had been knotted and reknotted. The sails were tattered and patched. The hull leaked. And where was the *Discovery*?

Finally on January 6, the *Resolution* lookout sighted the topsails of the *Discovery*. Clerke, now much weakened, was rowed to the *Resolution*. Ledyard and the others heard his wracking horrible coughing. His skin was gray. He seemed frail and impossibly thin as he was helped aboard. He kept up his regular witty banter, but anyone could tell he was failing—just like Anderson in the last days. No one said as much, but they probably wondered if Clerke would even be aboard for the final push north.

Compared to the joking, indefatigable Clerke, Cook seemed irritable and dour. He knew that they had to find safe anchorage to refit and replenish supplies—and soon. They could not afford to miss another season into the arctic.

Finally on January 17, 1779, after Bligh went out and tested the water's

A steep volcanic cliff lines one side of Kealakekua Bay, where the Resolution *and* Discovery *moored in Hawaii.*

depth with a smaller boat, Cook directed the ships into the middle of a harbor on the west side of the island of Hawaii. The morning was fine and pleasant. For once the winds had died down. Kealakekua Bay, meaning "path of the gods," was described by Ledyard as "commodious." Protected in all directions except the southwest, the bay seemed to be a perfect, safe place to anchor.

On the eastern side of the bay rose a steep black volcanic cliff. At its base was a narrow beach. Several small villages nestled among coconut palm-groves on the bay's south side. Near the cliff was an odd-looking rectangular structure made of wooden poles and a platform that stood nearly eighteen feet tall. To the north was a rock pool with fresh water at low tide.

Almost immediately, the ships were surrounded by an estimated one thousand canoes loaded with people, hogs, plantains, and sugarcane. "There were upon an average six persons at least in each canoe," wrote Ledyard, who was unusually sober in his estimate.

As many as ten thousand men, women, and children arrived. Some came in canoes. Others swam holding floats or without floats. They scrambled up the sides and hung by the hundreds around the outside of the ships. Meanwhile, the crowd on shore became a frenzied mob. Neither Ledyard nor any-one else on board had ever seen anything like it.

The sounds, sights, and smells of their hysterical welcome, Ledyard said, was "one of the most tumultuous and the most curious prospects that can be imagined." Men's shouts of joy mixed with the shrill cries of women, who danced and clapped and sang. Children screamed and laughed. Canoes tipped and splashed. Hogs squealed. The water churned under so many feet, so many arms.

Clearly, the natives must have heard about the strange ships' riches from the natives who had ventured out in canoes while the *Resolution* and *Discovery* were "hovering round the island." They had plenty of chance to get a grand welcome ready.

"I have no where in this Sea," Cook wrote, "seen such a number of people assembled at one place, besides those in the Canoes all the Shore of the bay was covered with people and hundreds were swimming about the Ships like shoals of fish."

In only moments, the crew had gone from famine to feast. They were sur-rounded by mountains of food—everything the island had to offer to eat. They glutted themselves on roast pig, fresh baked fish, baked sweet plantains, breadfruit, and boiled sweet potatoes. Women swarmed every corner of the ships. The deck was so crowded, no one could move. The natives brought such heaps of produce and roasted pigs, half of the bounty had to be taken away. There simply wasn't room.

In this wild, ecstatic crowd, the inevitable occurred. A bunch of keys van-ished. Backstay tackles, iron hooks, thimbles, lids of cooking pans disap-peared. An underwater swimmer busily pried nails from copper sheathing.

Cook was determined to set an example. He ordered the marines to shoot off one of the cannons, followed by two muskets to be fired with nonlethal small shot over natives in a canoe speeding away with a stolen boat rudder. "A good opertunity," Cook said, "to shew them the use of fire arms." When the blast occurred, the natives were "rather more surprised than frightened."

Others claimed the natives looked astonished. It turned out to be a waste of shot. The rudder was never retrieved.

The hysteria and chaos might have turned into an actual riot if it hadn't been for the iron fists of Parea and Kanina, subchiefs of the king. These two Hawaiian officials helped clear the decks. Next, Koa, an impressive holy man, was carefully lifted onto the *Resolution*. Koa was an ancient high priest of the island. The other natives clearly feared and respected the small, unattractive man. High Priest Koa's peeling skin and shaking body were ravaged from constantly drinking an intoxicant made from kava roots.

High Priest Koa introduced himself with much ceremony and wrapped a red cloth around Cook's shoulders. Then he handed him a pig. No one could understand exactly what the Hawaiians were saying.

In Cook's journal, he described briefly what happened next. That afternoon, he said, "I went a shore to view the place." He was accompanied in the pinnace by Ledyard and some of the other marines. They came without guns, Ledyard remembered. The only weapon Cook carried was a short ceremonial sword he wore as part of his official uniform.

The priests waved two upright long white poles toward the Hawaiians in canoes. On the beach the native crowd became quiet compared to the rowdy mob on the ships.

"Orono! Orono!" the crowd chanted. They bowed and covered their faces with their hands until Cook had passed. Ledyard observed with amusement how the people tried to avert their eyes from Cook's presence when he moved his head to look around. Like one giant being, the crowd dropped on all fours, their arms outstretched on the ground in front of them. And then, as soon as Cook passed, the natives leaped to their feet to follow him.

Cook, his attendants, and the marine guards were headed for the large *morai,* or sacred place, located a short distance north of the middle point of the bay. The *morai* was a rectangular black block approximately 20 by 40 yards in size. It was surrounded by a rickety wooden fence decorated with twenty human skulls and grinning wooden images carved from wood. Inside the fenced area was the *heiau,* a wooden scaffold surrounded by a dozen more images in a semicircle. An altar had been decorated with sacrificial offerings—heaps of fruit and the remains of a fly-bloated hog.

In the last line of his journal Cook wrote, "As soon as we landed, Touahah

*Cook (third from left near fence) was treated as a godlike high chieftain by the Hawaiians,
who are shown here giving him a special offering. The officers depicted surrounding
Cook probably include King, Gore, and Clerke.*

[Koa] took me by the hand and conducted me to a large Morai, the other
gentlemen with Parea and four or five more of the Natives followed."

The priests conducted a long, exhausting ceremony that neither Cook
nor his men understood. Cook, who had been through many ceremonies in
Tahiti and elsewhere, "was quite passive and suffered Koa to do with him as he
chose," King noted. A small pig was made into an offering over a fire. Cook
was directed to climb up the scaffolding, where he was ceremoniously
wrapped in a red cloth. Another hog was dashed to the ground.

Cook descended and was led about to the various statues. His face, hands, arms, and shoulders were rubbed with a cloth dipped in coconut that had been thoroughly chewed by one of the high priests. The decaying hog was cut into pieces and offered to Cook to eat. He tried to appear amiable but refused to swallow it, even when one of the other priests politely chewed the meat for him.

Cook, who remained baffled by a series of events on the scaffolding, had his own request. Could the priests provide him with a place on shore where the crowd wouldn't trample his astronomer's tents or steal his equipment? The priests gladly gave him a field of sweet potatoes near the *heiau*, which they made a motion to taboo. The taboo meant, they said, that no natives would be allowed to enter the area marked by white sticks. Cleverly, the priests also said that part of the bargain was that the men inside the tabooed area would not be allowed to cross the boundary either.

Cook agreed and went back to the ship.

Differences in language created a real problem. Although many of the men knew Tahitian, which was in many ways similar to the language of Hawaii, they had no knowledge of religious symbols or ideas behind the ceremony that had just occurred. "We could not understand a word," Ledyard admitted.

Little did Ledyard or the rest of the crew realize that Cook had just been welcomed as a supernatural being, possibly a reincarnation of the god *Orono Makua*. American missionary writers and native historians almost one hundred years later would first describe the connection between Cook and Orono, also known as Lono, the Hawaiian god of the season of plenty and leisure. Orono was said to move clockwise about the islands this time of year. He was to be greeted wherever he went with white banners.

In the eyes of the Hawaiians, Cook's lengthy clockwise circling of the island to trade; his arrival at the peak of the *mahiki* season or time of abundance at Kealakekua, "the path of the gods"; and his amazing ship with enormous white bannerlike sails pointed to some kind of miracle. Surely this strange white visitor distributing fantastic gifts was Orono, whose return had been foretold.

Chapter 14

VENTURING PAST THE BOUNDARY

From Hawaii and Back Again
January–February 1779

Ledyard was among the seven marines assigned to guard the tents on shore inside the tabooed area. They were told to keep in proper uniform and act like soldiers for once. Cook specifically ordered them "to keep up a respect amongst the People & not let the Natives handle their Pieces, or to shew them the Method of loading," King remembered.

At first everything seemed to work out fine. The people poured in by the hundreds and sat on the walls surrounding the *heiau* to watch the strangers with their odd, gleaming instruments pointed toward the sky. No one dared venture past the boundary. Ledyard felt grateful, fearing that their immense numbers might otherwise "trample me to attoms." Peace and order prevailed.

It was soon clear, however, that guarding the tabooed area had its drawbacks. Ledyard recognized this after only a few nights. Now that they were in paradise, the marines wanted to have some fun. Everyone else in the crew was. Why shouldn't they? The marines complained officially to their officers, who knew that Cook would never permit them to leave their stations.

In the darkness, however, a few marines secretly crept over the forbidden boundary to meet their girlfriends, who had stood on the boundary taunting them.

It wasn't long before the men and their officers passed one another in the night. They winked and pretended they hadn't seen one another.

But the chiefs weren't so unobservant or forgiving. They knew immediately that the taboo was being broken by Cook's men. Although Cook seemed to be treated like some sort of god, the crew members were certainly not behaving in a supernatural fashion. Ledyard predicted that as soon as the natives figured out that the white guards were as human as anyone else, "our situation would ruin us. . . . For my own part, I really foresaw the mischiefs that would ensue. . . . It was the beginning of our subsequent misfortunes."

Little by little, a more relaxed atmosphere crept into the tabooed area guarded by Ledyard and the other marines. The white poles vanished. Natives crisscrossed at their leisure. Now they could observe the strangers in their tents. They spied on "our conduct in private and unguarded hours," Ledyard said. They watched the marines wash their faces and their hands and eat their food. The natives set up informal boxing matches and saw how the strangers could be defeated. In only a short amount of time, it became abundantly clear that Ledyard and the other marines were just ordinary men.

The eventual breakdown of the taboo created temptations for theft—a situation that would only come to no good.

Meanwhile, Cook and his officers awaited the arrival of the highest king, whose name was Terreeoboo and who was said "to keep his subjects in great awe." On January 26, 1779, a battalion of the biggest canoes Ledyard and the others had ever seen paddled into the bay. The seventy-foot-long canoe held the king, who wore a bright yellow-and-red cape and a feathered helmet.

The king was escorted by assorted chiefs and priests in colorful feathered cloaks. Several other canoes were mounted with giant heads woven from baskets and decorated with red, green, and black feathers, oyster-shell eyes, and wide, vicious mouths studded with dogs' teeth. The king signaled for Cook to come ashore for the ceremonies. The captain got into the pinnace with help from the disheveled marines and was rowed to the beach. The plan was to meet in the astronomer's tent.

Ledyard was impressed by the king, an old man whom he described as "very feeble, about 5 feet 8 inches high, and of slender make." He had an

The enormous Hawaiian double canoes belonging to the chiefs measured nearly seventy feet in length—"the largest we had ever seen," according to Ledyard.

expressive face "of conscious dignity." Others found him slightly repulsive. Like many other high-status Hawaiians, the king was a heavy user of kava.

The king and his chiefs were fascinated by the strangers' powerful weapons that appeared to spew fire. "They had heard what terrible things our guns were," Ledyard wrote. The chiefs seemed to assume that the telescopes pointing toward the sky were some kind of lethal destroyers.

Rumors circulated around the island that the strangers spent an enormous time staring into the sky at the moon and sun. Did that mean that they controlled the heavens? Or were they originally from beyond the stars? Having never encountered white people before, the chiefs told their visitors that "the colour of our skins partook of the red from the sun, and the white from the moon and stars," Ledyard said.

Later Ledyard and the other sailors watched with amusement when the king, his chiefs, and servants inspected the *Resolution*. They measured its width and length, climbed aloft into the foretop, and scurried into the hold. Over and over they expressed utmost admiration. As excellent canoe craftsmen themselves, their obvious praise was taken as a great compliment by the ships' carpenters.

Ledyard and the others enjoyed sumptuous feasts and entertainment. "We live now in the greatest Luxury," Samwell admitted. The Hawaiians prepared enormous meals of baked hog and potatoes. Handsome native women performed graceful dances. Hawaiians sang complicated melodies accompanied by the beat of drums. They hosted boxing matches and athletic demonstrations.

The sailors tried to counter their hosts' generous entertainment with solos on a violin, flute, and French horn. The marines went through regimental drills, marching awkwardly as usual. As a grand finale, Cook ordered the last of their fireworks set off. These explosive displays on the beach terrified the natives so badly that they fled in terror. Cook laughed and laughed. The king, though not amused, managed to keep his composure through the unnerving event.

On January 26, the very day of the arrival of King Terreeoboo, Ledyard formally requested permission to explore farther inland and climb Mauna Loa, the snowcapped 13,680-foot peak that rose about twenty miles east of Kealakekua Bay. Perhaps he recalled his moment of triumphant return in Unalaska. Perhaps he longed for some kind of memorable greatness.

Cook agreed to Ledyard's request. That very afternoon, Ledyard set out with twenty-two-year-old George Vancouver, midshipman on the *Discovery;* David Nelson, botanical collector and servant to Bayly, the *Discovery* astronomer; Robert Anderson, gunner on the *Resolution;* and Simeon Woodruff, American-born gunner's mate on the *Discovery.*

They took no guns. Each man carried salted pork, a woolen blanket for the colder weather in higher altitudes, and a bottle of brandy for refreshment. Also joining them were three native men, who had never climbed a mountain before and had no idea where they were going. They refused to carry anything.

Another native they met along the way was appalled by their plan. He tried to convince them to go back. You'll never make it, he warned. He walked with them for a few miles before returning to his own village.

LEFT:
Hawaiian dancer with feathered gourd rattle

BELOW:
Hawaiian artifacts, including ceremonial mask, rattles, and horns. Shown center, below is a pahoa, *or iron dagger.*

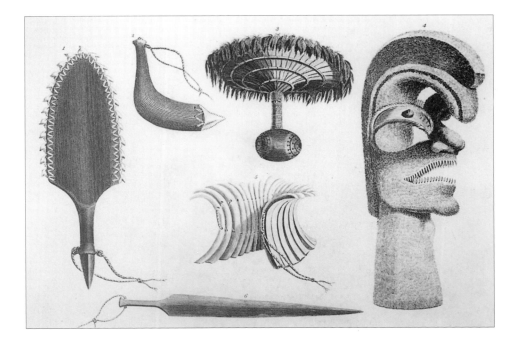

Ledyard led the ragtag, slow-moving group of sailors-turned-hikers, who were clearly more at home at sea than on land. Every so often the men stopped to collect a new plant or shoot at birds. Ledyard was fascinated by the change in terrain. He noted the plantations growing sweet potatoes and sugarcane. There were plantain trees and fields of grass. The land rose gradually and then became abruptly steep. Now there were breadfruit trees. Beyond that the land was crowded with lush ferns and woods with enormous trees.

After only four or five miles on the trail, they decided to spend the night in a native hut. Their hosts were an old couple and their young daughter. In his own inimitable style, Ledyard described the girl as "the emblem of innocent uninstructed beauty."

Ledyard and his companions sat outside the hut and stared down into the bay. In the distance they could see the beach, beyond that the ships, and beyond that the breathless blue ocean and neighboring islands. It was a quiet moment just before sunset. Surrounded by so much peace and natural beauty, Ledyard was speechless. That evening they bought a small pig from their host and had it for dinner with brandy diluted with mountain water, "a kind of nectar to us," Ledyard said.

That night the air felt chilly. Rain fell. The next day they set off on the wet, miry path that headed uphill. They used a compass to keep track of the mountain, but still managed to get themselves lost. "We had been unused to walking," Ledyard admitted, "especially to carrying such loads as we had." The natives continued to refuse to carry anything and complained they were tired. They were cold, the Hawaiians said. They wanted to go home.

The sun had not set, but they decided to stop for the day to allow time for botanizing and bird hunting. Ledyard concentrated on improving their camp-site, a fallen tree that lay four feet off the ground. He leaned pieces of bark and boughs on each side to make a shelter.

The next morning they set out in good spirits. They hoped to reach the snowy peak that day. Unfortunately, they had not even gone a mile when the path took a turn in the wrong direction, then vanished. Now what? Their water was gone. What should they do?

They discussed their options and decided to set out through the woods, going in the direction they thought the mountain was located. Every so often, one of the men climbed a tree to see where they were. After four miles trudging straight up through what Ledyard called "an impenetrable thicket," they changed their minds and returned to their original track. They ended up back at their campsite.

They shot some more lively birds with beautiful, wild plumage, trapped a few interesting insects, and measured trees with enormous twenty-foot girths. They'd given up on mountain climbing but decided to spend their time looking for interesting plants in the dense forest. Nelson hoped to collect some rare species for the Kew Gardens, in England.

High in the trees they heard the muffled bark of the native owl of Hawaii. *Pueo*, the natives told them. Everywhere they looked they saw quarrelsome, bright birds soaring over treetops. Birds with blood-red plumage were called *arapane*. Others, entirely green with a tinge of yellow, were musically named *amakihi*.

The next evening Ledyard, "being unwell, left them & returned to the tents," King later wrote. Ledyard mentioned nothing of this in his account. He only recorded that the group had walked perhaps twenty miles and returned on the evening of January 29. "Our Indians were extremely fatigued," said Ledyard, who could not have helped thinking of the expedition as a failure compared to his earlier venture. Next time, he vowed, he would travel light.

The visit to Hawaii began as a time of "constant exchange of good offices, & mutual little acts of friendship" between the sailors and the native people, Trevenen wrote. A group of children helped to save several sailors whose canoe tipped in the surf. The shouting children signaled to the men, showing them a way to safety. Ledyard himself was involved in his own minor rescue mission when an elderly woman fell into the water and had to be helped ashore.

Soon, however, the atmosphere at Kealakekua Bay began to change. Nearly every day thefts were reported: assorted knives, forks, and pewter plates that belonged to Second Lieutenant Phillips of the marines, as well as a carving knife from the *Resolution* gun room. The Hawaiians continued to bring great heaps of sugarcane, butchered hogs, and yams to the ships. But now they were trying to find out the strangers' plans. "When are you leaving?" King Terreeoboo asked Cook after yet another feast.

On February 1, 1779, William Watman, the *Resolution*'s ailing quarter gunner, died. A veteran of two earlier voyages with Cook, Watman had been sick for a while. Ledyard blamed his heavy drinking for his eventual death. Cook was fond of the old man and had promised to bury him on shore with pomp and circumstance near the *heiau*.

The news of the white man's death seemed to surprise the natives. Ledyard noticed that as soon as they brought the body ashore from the ship, all the local people hid in their houses. The marines marched in a funeral procession accompanied by a fife. Cook and his officers read prayers. Only one Hawaiian priest, Kikinny, was present during the actual burial. Just as the body was lowered into the ground, the priest seized a little pig by its hind legs, beat its head against the stones, and threw the lifeless body into the grave.

Cook and the marines marched away. A post was later erected on the site. Afterward Ledyard noticed how the natives came to the place and threw animal flesh on the grave. "They seemed," Ledyard said, "to pay a greater attention to this man's grave than that of their own people."

Later, while Ledyard was on evening guard duty, he saw a light glowing near the *heiau*. He went to investigate and found a group of about a dozen native men sitting around a fire in a circle. He recognized a few of the men. And they knew him. They called Ledyard by his nickname, Ourero. This may have been Ledyard's faulty recording of the Hawaiian *'olelo*, which means language or speech—a good description of chatty Ledyard. The Hawaiians invited Ledyard to sit down and join them. It was a serious gathering.

Ledyard did not know what was going on and was afraid at first to ask. After a half hour, someone killed a pig and threw its entrails into the fire. Then the carcass was pitched onto Watman's grave. Ledyard later thought the ceremony had something to do with sacrificing the spirit of the dead for Watman. Clearly, the death had unnerved the Hawaiians. If their visitors were godlike, how could they die?

The day of Watman's death, Cook issued an order to collect firewood. Timber from the woods was far away and difficult to transport. He inquired about the wooden fence that surrounded the *heiau*. What about buying the whole thing?

The natives seemed open to an offer from King, whom they called Cook's son. They obviously liked King and did not want to disappoint him. (In fact, they liked him so much, they later tried to convince him to stay behind in Hawaii after the ships left.) When King returned to Cook and told him that the high priests had agreed to the sale, the sailors went immediately to work breaking down the fence and loading the wood into the boats. For good measure, they gathered up most of the sacred carved images. No use leaving these souvenirs behind, they told one another.

The other priests were outraged. They had never agreed to Cook's price. To them, the sailors' destruction of their sacred statues was a desecration. A tragedy. Worse yet, Cook refused to recognize what a terrible sacrilege had taken place.

"Cook was insensible of the daily decline of his greatness and importance in the estimation of the natives," Ledyard wrote. "So confident was he, and so secure in the opposite opinion . . . that he offered [the two priests] two iron

Second Lieutenant James King, a year older than Ledyard, had joined the navy at age twelve. He studied at Oxford and was a competent astronomer.

hatchets. The chiefs were astonished not only at the inadequate price, but at the proposal and refused him."

While the fence was being carted away, the Hawaiians stood outside the walls of the *heiau* and watched with angry expressions. Ledyard and the other guards packed up their belongings from the tabooed area and took them back to the ship. As soon as they were gone and the priest lifted the taboo from the area, the natives swarmed the place in search of nails or anything else left behind.

A few days later, a mysterious fire broke out near the place where the astronomer's tents had been located. A little after dark, two old houses that stood on the corner of the *morai* burned down. One structure had been used by sail makers to repair some canvas. Another nearby building had been used as a hospital. At first Ledyard and the others thought the fire was due to carelessness. "But it was not the case," Ledyard said. "The natives burnt it themselves, to shew us the resentment they entertained toward us."

Not surprisingly the natives appeared glad to see the ships prepare for departure early in the morning of February 4, 1779. The *Resolution* and *Discovery* unmoored and sailed out of the bay. They had plenty of salted pork and food, but they still needed water. The plan was to head for Oahu, heading north to finish circling the island of Hawaii for the charts. The day was clear and fine.

In less than two days, however, a squall hit. For the next thirty-six hours, the storm raged. On February 8, the foremast of the *Resolution* split. And then they lost contact with the *Discovery*. The "irregular sea," Ledyard wrote, "was such as demanded our best skill and unremitted attention to keep the ship under any kind of command."

The treacherous direction of the wind and current meant that there was nowhere to go but back the way they had come to Kealakekua Bay. Cook was exhausted and angry. Privately, he cursed the corrupt Deptford Naval Yards. He cursed his patrons, who had benefited financially from such shoddy work.

Kealakekua Bay was the only place they could go to make repairs. Everyone knew they had overstayed their welcome. But they seemed to have no choice. On February 11, they arrived back in the bay.

The place was eerily silent. The natives had given as much as they possibly could in the way of supplies. No one came out in clamoring throngs to greet them. The stillness was unnerving and humiliating. "Our return to this bay was as disagreeable to us," Ledyard said, "as it was to the inhabitants, for we were reciprocally tired of each other."

Cook ordered the sails to be hauled down. The yards and topmast were removed. The marines went ashore to help set up a workshop for repairs. Ledyard helped set up the astronomer's tent for the telescopes and clocks. This was erected in the same place they had been located before on the *morai*—the same place where the houses had been burned. Ledyard and six other marines were to stay on shore as guards.

A lone canoe appeared, bearing a fierce chief in a red-feathered cloak. His name was Kamehameha and he said he was the king's nephew. He came paddling out to tell Cook and Clerke that the king was gone. The priests had tabooed the bay until his return. Kamehameha signaled that he'd sell his cloak. His price, he said, was nine *pahoa*, or iron daggers.

Why nine? Clerke demanded suspiciously.

Kamehameha wouldn't say. He hurried away.

By nightfall canoes reappeared in the bay. The easy bartering for plantains, coconuts, and hogs had clearly ended. The natives' prices, the sailors found, had skyrocketed. What alarmed Ledyard most of all was the way the natives kept asking for the same item of trade: *pahoa*. "It was also equally evident from the looks of the natives as well as every other appearance that our former friendship was at an end."

Chapter 15

"Our Father Is Gone"
Hawaii
February 1779

Kealakekua Bay, which once had the look of paradise to Ledyard and the other men, now bore instead the eerie resemblance to an open, fanged jaw.

The distance from Kaawaloa, the bay's far northwest land point (the front tooth), to Palemano Point, the far southwest point (the bottom tooth), was only one and one-quarter mile. When the *Resolution* and *Discovery* returned to the bay, the ships anchored where they had before, opposite the steep black volcanic cliff, or *pali*. At the edge of this cliff was a narrow beach, a rough lava lip that met the water.

The ships rested about a quarter mile from shore in 13 fathoms of water. The *Resolution* was moored to the north, the *Discovery* to the south, opposite the *heiau*, near the village called Waipunaula.

On shore near the center of the bay was the watering place and a village called Kealakekua. To the south of this village was the *heiau*, where the astronomer's observatory tent was set up once again. It was here that Ledyard and the other marines were stationed to guard the carpenters who worked on replacing the end or heel of the foremast, which was discovered to have rotted with a hole "large enough to hold a coconut." To the south of Ledyard's encampment were three other native villages within sight of the shore.

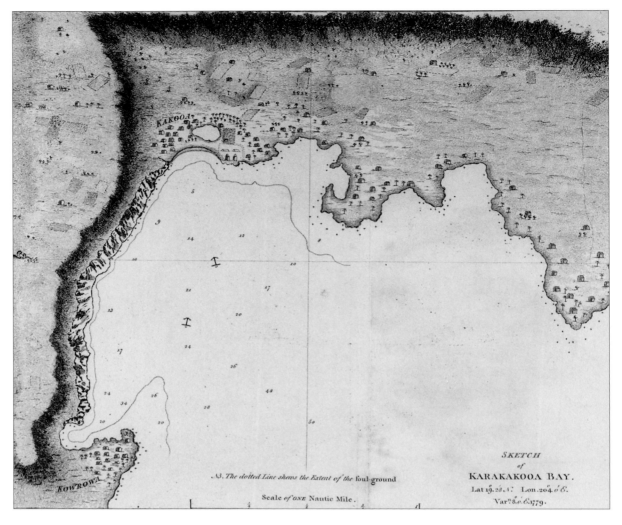

Sketch of Kealakekua Bay (called Karakakooa Bay by Cook's crew)

The bay echoed with the sounds of work crews hastily finishing repairs. Although the bay was not large, communication was difficult between groups left on the ships and spread out in various places on shore.

On the afternoon of February 13, an unarmed group from the *Discovery*, out collecting water, rolled casks onto the shore near Kealakekua village. The natives' "passive appearance of disgust" that Ledyard noticed when they arrived quickly changed into something more ominous. Instead of lending a hand the way they had in the past, native men with protective, woven-grass mats over their bodies skulked among the trees. They hurled insults and pitched rocks.

Terrified, William Hollamby, *Discovery* quartermaster in charge, rushed to King, who was with Ledyard and the other marines at the observatory near the *heiau,* where the mast was being repaired. Hollamby complained that an estimated one hundred "very troublesome" natives were gathered near the village. King marched north along the beach with a marine armed with a musket. He went into the trees, found the chief, and threatened him with a musket if he didn't call off the mob. Amazingly, his bold move worked. The crowd drifted away.

When King returned to the observatory, he arrived in time to see Cook splashing ashore from the pinnace. He had come to inspect the carpenters' work. King told his captain what had happened. Cook was furious. He ordered Ledyard and the others to load their muskets with deadly ball. Shoot to kill, Cook commanded. "Fire on the first appearance of any natives throwing stones or behaving insolently."

Suddenly, a musket shot echoed across the bay from the *Discovery.* Ledyard turned and watched a canoe paddling swiftly away from the ship. A boat was lowered from the *Discovery* and gave chase. Another theft! Cook signaled to King, a marine with a musket, and Corporal Ledyard to go with him. The four men loped up the rocky beach to try to intercept the paddler when he landed to the south. King sprinted ahead, but the canoe arrived before he could reach it. Cook, Ledyard, and the marine, red-faced and out of breath, made a humiliating dash through the village of Kealakekua.

Where is he? Cook demanded.

"Not here. Go south," the villagers told the men. The Hawaiians could barely conceal their amusement.

Cook fumed and raged at the natives. He threatened to shoot them. But no one would give him any information about where the thief might be hiding. "Try Kalama," the natives said, pointing to the village farther south.

Cook, Ledyard, King, and the other marine rushed to Kalama. "Try Kahuloa," the Kalama villagers said.

Everywhere Cook and his men went, natives surrounded them in ominous groups. Only when Ledyard or the other marine pointed their muskets did they stand back. After a while, however, the crowd "began to laugh at our

Captain James Cook as he appeared in 1776 before leaving on his last voyage.
This image is based on a portrait done from life by
Sir Nathaniel Dance.

threat," as King put it. No one called out for "Orono" when they saw Cook coming. There was no bowing, no groveling now. Hatred and contempt bubbled like hot lava just before an eruption.

"We shall never apprehend the rascal by this means," Cook shouted at King and the marines.

They finally reached Palemano Point, at the bay's southernmost tip. Cook, Ledyard, and the others had ended up three miles from the place they started, "highly displeased," Ledyard wrote, "and not a little concerned at the bad appearance of things. But even this was nothing to what followed."

Cook had worked himself up into a frenzy by the time they made their way back to their starting point at the observatory. It was dark. Cook was sweating heavily. He took off his jacket. King was in bad shape as well. He had an abscess on his chest that was causing him great pain.

Cook announced that he would give the crews a tongue-lashing for certain as soon as he got back on the ship. In the bay they could see that lanterns had been lit on the *Resolution* and the *Discovery*. Cook was taken to the ships while Ledyard and the other exhausted marine stayed ashore to continue guarding the mast and the observatory tent.

Only later did Ledyard find out what had happened that afternoon. A native boldly snatched a pair of tongs and a chisel from the blacksmith's forge, then dived off the *Discovery*. A volley of shot missed the swimmer, who jumped into a waiting canoe. The canoe was paddled swiftly across the bay and landed on shore, where the thief vanished. The wild-goose chase along the beach had only been an amusement for the villagers.

While Ledyard, King, and Cook were on their hopeless chase, another fight had broken out farther up the beach. The scuffle was over the pinnace. Two unarmed men, *Discovery* Master Thomas Edgar and Midshipman George Vancouver, neither of whom could swim, decided to try and protect the boat from natives who were quickly pulling it apart for iron. They would have been stoned to death if a chief had not stepped in and stopped the riot.

That evening Cook announced gravely to King that everything had changed. "The behavior of the Indians obliges me to use force," he said. All the natives still on board the *Resolution* were told to get off, including the women.

Meanwhile, King went ashore to tell Ledyard and the marines their new instructions as they guarded the mast and astronomer's tent. "If you see any Indians lurking about at any distance, call to me," King said. "If any should approach so close as to leave it in no doubt that their intentions were bad, fire without orders."

It was an uneasy night for Ledyard and the other marines. Clearly, the spell of their imaginary greatness had been broken. They had superior weapons but were outnumbered. A musket could only be loaded so quickly. A thousand natives with rocks might easily overpower them. And then what would they do?

In the darkness, branches broke. Leaves crunched. Five figures scurried past. The marine on duty grabbed his musket. In his haste, he fired. More footsteps. Anyone hurt? No. Ledyard listened hard. Whoever had tried to approach had hurried away unharmed. The rest of the sleepless night, Ledyard and the others sat uneasily, watching, waiting. But no one else bothered them.

The next morning dawned with fine weather and gentle sea breezes. Almost immediately an alarm went up. The cutter, a small boat with a sail that had been moored near the *Discovery,* had been stolen right from under the crew's noses in the night.

Cook was told immediately. For once, he did not go into a rage. We'll make a trap, he said. The boats will position themselves in the bay and will hold all canoes hostage that attempt to escape. The blockade will remain in effect until the cutter is returned. "We shall fire our great guns if it should prove necessary," Cook told Clerke.

From shore, Ledyard and the other marines could sense that something had shifted. Something dangerous. From nearby they heard the worried voices of women and children as they quickly gathered up their belongings and headed inland to safety.

Out in the bay Ledyard could see boats filled with armed men being lowered from the ships. At the same time, farther north, war canoes were being hastily launched. Cannon fire blasted from the *Resolution* in the direction of the shore. The shot arched and splashed in the water.

Meanwhile, one of the *Resolution*'s cutters filled with ten armed men—no marines—under the direction of Bligh. The men pointed their guns toward the approaching war canoe. Bligh stood and signaled. Gunfire echoed across the bay. Smoke rose.

The terrified natives leaped into the water. Those remaining in the canoe turned and paddled toward shore. The canoe was quickly abandoned.

Ledyard and the others cheered. They watched in eager anticipation. Ledyard longed for a fight. This was his chance. He would do his part. He would make a name for himself.

But Ledyard and the marines had no signal to begin firing. They could not

Master William Bligh, painted by John Chapman many years after the return of the Resolution. *Bligh managed to survive two mutinies, in 1789 and 1808, and became an admiral.*

do anything except stay where they were, guarding the observatory tent. Time passed. It was maddening waiting for something to happen.

The *Resolution* lowered another boat. Ledyard and the others peered into the distance and watched what was certainly the captain, resplendent in his uniform and hat. He was coming ashore with what looked like Marine Second Lieutenant Phillips, Sergeant Gibson, Corporal Thomas, and seven privates. Damn their eyes! Ledyard impatiently watched the boat rowing methodically to the north toward the landing place at Kaawaloa.

The pinnace with the captain pulled ashore. Another of the ship's small craft lay in the shallows, waiting. Cook, stooped but taller than all the ragtag group shouldering muskets, got out of the boat. He marched resolutely over the black lava rocks, through the trees toward the center of the village of Kaawaloa. Soon they were out of sight.

They were followed ashore by King, who landed near the *heiau*. He pulled his small cutter ashore and headed directly toward the place where Ledyard, the other marines, the carpenters, the astronomer, and the sail makers anxiously awaited news.

Well, now at least they could find out what they were going to do. What kind of action was in store for them?

But when King arrived, he informed Ledyard and the others of the captain's plan. Gore was to remain aboard the *Resolution*. Clerke was too sick to move. Cook had gone ashore with the marines to locate the hut of Kalei'opu'u, an important chief. They planned to take him hostage until the cutter was returned. King shook his head as if he believed the plan to bring the old king back against his will foolhardy—especially with a thousand warriors massing all along the bay.

Ledyard had other questions. What if the king wasn't there? What if he had already escaped?

"'Occupy the morning burning houses and seizing canoes.' That's what the captain said," King replied.

Destroying innocent native, property didn't sound very glorious. What were Ledyard and the other marines supposed to do in the meantime?

"Remain together. Keep on guard," King told him. "Post your men with muskets loaded with ball. Open fire under provocation."

This was not the news that Ledyard wanted to hear. While Gibson, Thomas, and their group were on a glory mission, he was trapped there—bored and useless. The carpenters did a bit of work. The muskets were checked, stacked, checked again. Ledyard and the other marines in bright red uniforms marched back and forth, always keeping a watchful eye toward the water. Several boats and cutters moved back and forth, trying to keep the canoes inside the bay.

Minutes crawled by. Still nothing seemed to happen. In the distance the *Resolution* cutter, with Williamson at the helm, bobbed in the waves off shore near the place where the captain had landed. A startling explosion of cannonfire blasted from the *Resolution*. Ledyard and the others watched Bligh's boat take off in pursuit of another war canoe.

It was ridiculous just waiting here, helpless. Watching the confusion. Not understanding anything yet being unable to act because of orders.

Another burst of musket fire echoed, this time from nearby Waipunaula. Ledyard and the marines dived for cover. Out in the bay close together bobbed the *Discovery* launch and small cutter. Smoke hung overhead. Another double canoe escaped. Meanwhile a small canoe with four natives approached the *Discovery*. Another group of natives rushed up the shore toward Kaawaloa.

And suddenly the air was filled with the ominous sound of conch shells being blown. A warning. Faint cries came from across the bay, where thousands of natives waved clubs and spears and poured out onto the beach from between the trees. They swarmed as dense and dark as a horde of fish. A pack of sharks.

Something had gone wrong. Very wrong.

Through the telescope Ledyard and the others could see a glint of bright white-and-red uniform. A volley of musket fire. A puff of smoke. Another shot. Another volley. The crush of people moved toward the water, into the water. Bodies so thick, so close together it was impossible to see anything.

Where was Cook?

Ledyard held his breath and watched. Twenty seconds to reload. He knew that was all the time the marines on shore would have. Twenty seconds.

Silence.

The water frothed white with splashing. A hail of stones flew through the air. Men in red uniforms plunged into the water as if making for the boats. The crowd roared.

The pinnace came closer to shore. Something big and heavy was heaved over into the boat. The pinnace rowed furiously toward the *Resolution*. The ship opened fire, sending balls into the crowd. Panicked sounds of screams. People scattered. Another launch turned toward shore, paused, then pulled oars and returned to the safety of the middle of the bay.

Ledyard watched as if in a dream, half-expecting the crowd to turn and come toward them, destroy all of them, every last one. But the natives slipped into the trees. The bay was suddenly, eerily silent.

In less than an hour and a half, everything had changed. Even at this distance from the main action, cut off from the two ships, Ledyard, King, and the others could sense that something irrevocable had happened.

"Boats were passing between the Ships," King observed. "All fyring had ceas'd, & we for about 10 minutes or a quarter of an hour, were under the most torturing suspence & anxiety that can be conceiv'd. I never before felt such agitation as on seeing at last our Cutter coming on shore, with Mr. Bligh."

Without saying a word, they could tell from Bligh's grim expression. Cook was dead.

Bligh signaled to his men to disembark from the cutter. They were heavily armed with muskets and pistols and cutlasses. Among the reinforcements was pale Phillips, bandaged and silent.

Bligh bustled about in his take-charge way. Cook was murdered, he told Ledyard and the others. Corporal Thomas and Privates Theophilus Hinks, John Allen, Thomas Fatchett. All marines. All dead. Their bodies, Bligh said, were still in the possession of the savages.

Ledyard and the others were too stunned to speak.

"Get ready to leave. Take everything," Bligh ordered. There was no time now for details.

King directed the furious activity as they gathered up the astronomical equipment, the tent, and the half-repaired mast. These would be loaded into the cutter and then onto the ship for safekeeping. As the men worked, they kept glancing over their shoulders toward the dark trees. Eyes. There might be someone watching, waiting in there. Maybe groups of stealthy natives gathering.

Before the men could finish loading the cutter, something rustled in the dry leaves. Footsteps thudded near the *morai* walls. Bligh ordered everyone under cover. Keep a lookout, he said.

For the next hour, Ledyard and the others watched and waited. *Clunk!* Someone chucked a rock. *Clunk!* Then another.

"There!" Bligh shouted, pointing beyond the walls. "Fire!"

"Mr. Bligh, are you—" Bayly protested. But the rest of the astronomer's words were drowned out in an explosion of marine gunfire. Bayly crouched and stuffed his fingers in his ears. His equipment. All his precious equipment was out there in the open about to be blown to pieces.

"Reload!" Bligh commanded. "Fire!"

Again and then again the muskets blasted. Almost machinelike, Ledyard loaded, aimed, fired. It was so easy under the protection of the *morai* walls to shoot down on the creeping, rock-throwing natives. As easy as hunting waterfowl with Gore.

Boom! Ledyard and the others looked up, startled. From the bay came the unmistakable roar of a cannon from the *Discovery*. A cannonball arched. It hit the beach, spraying sharp bits of sand and slivers of lava rock everywhere.

Ledyard instinctively crouched, terrified. He knew the *Discovery* was trying to help them. But there was always the chance the gunner might miss and blow the *morai*—and everyone hiding there—to pieces.

Bligh was first on his feet. Look at those savages, he crowed with satisfaction. They're running.

Sure enough, the wounded natives had limped down the beach into the trees. They left behind crumpled companions, sprawled bloody and motionless where they'd fallen. The cannon fire ceased. The only sound to be heard was the wailing of women hidden in the coconut grove.

Eight dead, Bligh said. Always one for accuracy, he counted again and looked pleased. He didn't regret his unauthorized action—the indiscriminate killing of natives. He felt sure that what he had done was right. If Cook and the other softhearted fools had listened to him about a show of force right from the start, he reasoned, none of this would ever have happened.

Ledyard stood up and glanced around in a daze. He had never killed anyone before. Not on purpose. He sniffed. The familiar deadly odor of gunpowder lingered in the air.

Bligh was congratulating them. Good work, he said.

Ledyard hardly heard Bligh. His thoughts were on the other side of the bay. Corporal Thomas, Privates Theophilus Hinks, John Allen, and Thomas

Many artists depicted the dramatic death of Captain James Cook (center slinging a musket). This popular image by George Carter shows the boats with Williamson and the marines much closer to shore than they were in real life.

Fatchett. *All marines. All dead. Their bodies still in the possession of the savages.* If not for Providence, Ledyard might have been among them. All he had to do was take one glance at Phillips' bloody shoulder. And he suddenly knew. Whatever brave deed Ledyard—or any of them—had done just now made no difference. Cook would never know. He was gone.

By noon, every piece of equipment had been gathered and hauled back to the ship. When Ledyard reboarded the *Resolution,* he was instantly aware of the sense of gloom and outrage of the other men. Some sobbed. Others wanted to blast all of Hawaii to bits. To kill everyone. The mixture of melancholy and violence pervaded the *Resolution* and the *Discovery.* For nearly half an hour no one spoke. "Grief was visible on every Countenance," Gilbert remembered.

Clerke, feeble and ravaged by illness, was in charge now. He could barely stand up on the *Resolution* deck. Gore, Ledyard's friend, had moved over to command the *Discovery.* Little by little, in talking to eyewitnesses and listening to gossip, Ledyard was able to piece together that fateful afternoon.

What he discovered was that Cook had gone into the village to take the old chief prisoner. The bewildered chief resisted but followed Cook toward the beach. His followers, alarmed by what was happening, came rushing toward the growing crowd with reports of another murder across the bay. Soon Cook was surrounded with spears and daggers.

The marines retreated toward the water's edge. Cook made his way slowly toward the water. He fired once when a man jumped him. The gun was loaded with shot and did not penetrate the mat vest he was wearing. Emboldened, the furious crowd tightened around Cook. A painful shower of stones pelted the men. A marine fell. Cook fired and killed a man. "Take to the boats!" Cook had cried.

Phillips was stabbed and knocked down. He shot his attacker. Then he managed to stumble back to his feet and keep moving toward the water. Corporal Thomas was stabbed and drowned. Privates Hinks, Allen, and Fatchett were hacked to pieces.

Cook, his gun empty now, turned and waved for the waiting boats to come closer. In that instant he was stabbed with a *pahoa* in the back, the most humiliating place of all for a Hawaiian warrior. Cook plunged face-first into the water and was held under until he drowned. Someone clobbered a rock against the back of his skull. His body was dragged off by the natives.

The news was worse than anything Ledyard could have imagined. "We have lost our father!" someone on the gangway whispered. "Our father is gone!"

Chapter 16

"AMPLE VENGEANCE"

From Hawaii to Avacha Bay
February–August 1779

It took the next four days for Clerke to cajole and threaten their few remaining friends in Hawaii to return the bodies of Cook and the marines. Cook's hands appeared, recognizable because of a scar. A hat. Part of a thigh wrapped in a cloth and a piece of skull that were stored in a box for eventual burial. The crew was reassured by the priest who had brought the box that they had been part of a Hawaiian ritual to honor the highest, greatest chiefs in this way. They were taunted with flags made from marine uniforms. Another native twirled Cook's hat around on a stick just out of musket range.

This only made the men aboard the *Resolution* white-hot with revenge.

On February 17, running low on water, a party was sent ashore with casks to collect water from the well. Ledyard and a group of marines landed on shore in two launches to guard the watering place as casks were rolled up the hill, filled, and hauled back to the ship. The place was eerily quiet at first. It wasn't long, however, before natives began pelting rocks through the trees and from behind houses. Since the well was located at the bottom of the hill, it was easy for large boulders to be rolled down on top of the men.

Clerke ordered an attack on the *heiau* to discourage the natives from gathering their forces and wiping out the group collecting water. Warning shots from *Discovery* cannons were fired. About fifty marines and sailors carrying torches, loaded muskets, and cutlasses volunteered as reinforcements under the command of Bligh. That evening they left for shore in cutters. Ledyard described how the marines enticed the hidden natives out of the houses on the beach and then exposed them to the "fire of the ship as well as our own."

Then the men joined into one column and marched into the village. Reportedly Bligh gave the order "to strike terror among them, by pursuing them with fire and sword."

In only a few moments all discipline fell apart. Roving groups of eager sailors set fire to thirty huts. They chopped up canoes. They shot men and women "wherever they met them," Gilbert wrote. Ledyard estimated, with obvious exaggeration, that the number killed was "near a hundred." Others who were in the massacre claimed the dead to be about a half dozen.

Stone throwers were hunted down, beaten, then shot. A group of unnamed sailors savagely cut the heads off two bodies, stuck the heads on poles, and paraded these up and down the beach. The heads were later fixed like trophies on the sterns of boats. These were viewed by some as "a terror to the enemy from ever daring again to molest us." When Clerke saw the heads, he immediately ordered them thrown overboard.

Huts were plundered of valuables. Spoils, including war clubs, bows, and arrows, were carried to the ships that night when the pillaging and arson ended. In the general desolation, it was fortunate that so many of the natives escaped into the hills with their lives. One old woman refused to leave her burning home. She was told to go to the beach for safety. She was terrified because she told them that she had two daughters on board the *Discovery* and what would become of them?

No sailors' lives were lost. "Our people in this days transactions did many reprehensible things," King wrote, "in excuse of which it can only be said that their minds were strongly agitated at the barbarous manner in which the Capt was treated; and they were very desirous of taking ample Vengeance."

The officers could not restrain the men, King said. Whether Ledyard tried to stop his marines' "ample Vengeance" does not seem likely. When he wrote his description of what happened in those hours, he neglected to reveal his emotions. He simply concluded his account with the statement: "Thus ended this days business."

The men who participated in this "business" undoubtedly had mixed feelings later about what they did. For Ledyard, the actions of February 17, 1779, would haunt him for years.

During the burning, shooting, and looting, Ledyard had followed the mob. There was nothing admirable about his actions. Yet the bravado he displayed may have been a desperate act of self-protection, an attempt to make sure that none of the other sailors would ever be able to accuse him of being a coward.

After all, he had seen firsthand what happened to mollycoddles and poltroons. Take Third Lieutenant Williamson of the *Resolution,* for example. Always unpopular, Williamson became openly despised and physically threatened by the other sailors after Cook's murder. Williamson was accused of cowardice when he failed to order the pinnace to rescue the Great Man during the natives' attack. The other tars made sure Williamson never lived down his shame.

Not until February 19 was the last of Cook's body collected. Cook's shoes and other pieces of clothing as well as his double-barreled gun, now badly mangled, were returned. Three days later, Cook's funeral took place on the *Resolution* with the crew from both ships present. At five o'clock the ships' flags were hoisted to half-mast.

Clerke, too frail to speak, had one of the other officers read the prayers. The men sang. The coffin was lowered over the side as the marines shot a ten-gun salute into the air. Except for the sound of surf, the bay was eerily quiet. The area had been tabooed and was deserted of any natives.

After the ceremony ended, Ledyard and the others heard rumors of the strange question Terreeoboo had asked King when he found out when the ships were leaving. "And when will Orono return?" he said nervously.

Before long, was King's cryptic reply.

On February 23, the ships weighed anchor and headed out of the bay toward the open water. For Ledyard and many of the other gloomy sailors, leaving their captain behind was deeply traumatic. Without the luck and know-how of Cook, "the Most Experienced and ablest navigator" among them, they had little hope of ever locating the fabled Northwest Passage, said Surgeon John Law, now of the *Resolution*. Quiet melancholy haunted the ship. "We left the bay . . . ," Ledyard wrote, "where [Cook] had acquired his honor, and in that spot where his exploits terminated."

Bad feeling festered among the crew. No one agreed who could be blamed for the disaster. Whatever the reason behind the tragedy, Ledyard felt he was the man to record the fateful event for future generations. "There is a moment to be seized on in all occasions," Ledyard once wrote.

Feeling that fate was on his side, he marched to Clerke's cabin and knocked on the door. He offered his services as "biographer" of the expedition. "I am no philosopher," Ledyard freely admitted. "However as a traveller and a friend to mankind I shall most freely relate any matter of curious facts to be improved by them."

Clerke smiled. What made this upstart American think he was a better writer than an educated, upper-class British gentleman? Did he know that nearly every other officer was keeping a journal? Ledyard nodded. Undaunted, he handed Clerke a writing sample, several pages describing the manners of the Society Islanders.

Clerke glanced through the papers and handed them back. Sorry, he said, barely concealing a smirk.

Ledyard withdrew. This exchange with the *Resolution*'s new captain did not improve Ledyard's low opinion of Clerke, whom he viewed as a priggish, condescending boor. It also didn't help that Ledyard overheard laughter as the story of his offer quickly circulated among the precious gentlemen. "[Ledyard's] ideas," Lieutenant James Burney later admitted, "were thought too sentimental and his language too florid."

Ledyard, always proud, was never one to suffer the fool.

Like everyone else, he knew that Clerke was dying. For the last several days, Clerke had been too weak to even come up on deck. How long would he last? No one knew. And yet Ledyard and the others were obligated to obey Clerke, who was determined to follow Cook's directions to the letter. The plan was to proceed north to examine "a narrow space between the two

Continents which was left unexplored last Year," Samwell grumbled, "tho' we have sufficient Reason from the shallowness of the Water, no Current & other Circumstances that there can be no Passage between them."

Ledyard and the other men feared going back into the terrible cold and dangerous ice. There weren't enough warm clothes or shoes. The ships, although repaired and patched repeatedly, were in need of a major overhaul with new rigging and sails. The flimsy, rotten sheathing would never hold up under penetrating ice conditions. The crew's spirits had never sunk so low. Some wondered if they'd ever see home again.

On March 1, running short of fresh water, Clerke ordered a special detour to Kauai to take casks to shore to be refilled. They knew of a place where they had found an especially fine rivulet, as Ledyard called it. Almost immediately, they met with difficulty. Everyone in Kauai had heard about the deaths at Kealakekua Bay. Nobody was impressed with these white strangers anymore.

"We had not only more wild uncivilized men to deal with, but an injured and exasperated people," Ledyard wrote. Not only had the inhabitants heard of Cook's death, the massacre afterward, and the burning of the town, but they also had other personal grievances. The venereal disease that the sailors had left behind on their first visit in 1778 had now become an epidemic on Kauai.

"The Venereal disease . . . had since made the most shocking ravages," wrote Ledyard, who had himself been infected at the time and may have been one of the contributors. "Our Seamen are in these matters so infernal and dissolute a Crew," King reflected on March 3, 1779, "that for the gratification of the present passion that affects them they would entail universal destruction upon the whole of the Human Species."

On March 1, Ledyard joined the small, armed watering party at Waimea Bay, on Kauai. For the next three days, they tried to roll empty casks to be filled in a fine rivulet. The natives turned surly. They hurled insults and gathered in threatening mobs, completely outnumbering the sailors. Thieving grew out of hand.

The marines formed a circle around the water collectors. When a native tried to cross the line, a marine gave him a poke with his bayonet. Immediately, tempers flared. What seemed at first like "a strange mixture of childishness and malice," King wrote, increasingly became something more serious.

A thief fled with a bag of nails. King ordered a marine to fire. Fortunately, he missed. The other marines splashed into the shallow water, took to their smaller boats, and headed back to the main ship. Left on shore were King, Robert Anderson, gunner, and John Grant, able seaman from the *Resolution*. King ordered Anderson and Grant to swim for their lives to the waiting pinnace, but neither would leave. It seemed to be a point of honor to be the last one on the beach. No one could forget Williamson's actions.

The natives pitched stones. King jumped in the water. He was followed by the two stragglers, who barely made it to the pinnace in time to be hauled on board. "The smallest error on our side might have been fatal to us," said King.

The incident at Waimea Bay was the beginning of a series of humiliating scrapes that nearly ended in disaster. It was as if the crews of the *Resolution* and the *Discovery* were being haunted by their own misdeeds.

On March 17, as soon as they left the Sandwich Islands and headed north for the arctic, strong gales and squalls hit. Water rushed into a new leak in the *Resolution*. Ledyard and the others manned the pumps. Then the winds turned contrary and uncertain and made it difficult to reach Kamchatka, in Asia.

Temperatures plummeted by April 6. There were barely enough jackets to go around. The sailors "begin to complain of the cold confoundedly," Clerke wrote. Landing in Kamchatka became critical. They were running out of food. The ropes were breaking so quickly they could not be repaired.

"Our clothing . . . was miserable," said Ledyard. "Our food was the same on Monday morning and Sunday evening—pork and yams begun, and pork and yams ended all our bills of fare." They were on half-rations and most of the yams were found to be rotten.

Cold, wet, and hungry, "we pumped and bailed her half the voyage," complained Ledyard, who was among the marines who had to work in shifts removing frigid water from the hold. Ice coated the rigging in some places "as thick as a man's thigh," King said, making it almost impossible to handle. Treacherous snow covered the deck. Fog blinded them. On April 13, another hard wind split the foresails and mizzen to pieces. More pumping. More bailing.

The *Discovery* disappeared from view. Even with an extra allowance of grog, life was miserable for Ledyard and the other sailors working nonstop to keep the ship afloat. The only dry place was Clerke's cabin, where he lay dying. Sail makers crowded into the captain's cramped quarters with their needles to mend the sails with the few scraps of canvas remaining. The men, King said, were "miserably pinched by cold." Many suffered from frostbite.

On April 26, in heavy snows and fog, the news only became worse. The chronometer, a clock used to calculate longitude, had stopped and would not restart. Now there was no way to be certain of their location.

Finally, three days later, they reached the harbor of Avacha, on the Kamchatka peninsula, with no sign of the *Discovery*. Sharp ice floated around them like a treacherous jigsaw puzzle. Those fortunate to escape the confines of the *Resolution* soon discovered it was nearly impossible to walk along the shore without falling through the ice into cold water up to one's armpits.

With great relief, the men watched the *Discovery* reappear and come to anchor in the harbor.

Fortunately for the expedition, a German-speaking Russian was discovered who could communicate with the expedition's painter, German-born John Webber. Clerke was able to buy desperately needed supplies on credit: twenty head of poor cattle, flour, some tobacco, tar, cordage, and canvas.

Ledyard and the rest of the crew helped cut firewood. They gathered water. Coopers worked on barrels. Carpenters repaired the ship's open seams and replaced rotten sheathing riddled by worms. Sail makers pieced together what they could of sails and rigging. Even at the end of April, Siberia seemed a miserable place. "All the country was coverd with Snow, & imagination could not paint a more dreary Prospect," King wrote. The men felt glad not to have spent the winter in a place with so little food, so much scurvy. On May 17, the carpenter's mate, Alexander McIntosh, died of flux, or diarrhea, and was buried at sea.

By May 13, enough greenery had appeared to improve the men's diet with "wild sellery, Garlick & Nettles" boiled with portable soup. The men aired

Desperate for supplies, the crew found unlikely help in the miserable village of Bolsheretsk in the Siberian wasteland. Major Behm, who lived there, generously provided flour, beef, and tobacco.

their bedding and smoked below decks, trying to keep up the routine that Cook had insisted upon. The men's only diversions were bear hunts, fishing trips, and occasional visits to the village to Kamchadal women, whom Ledyard found "indolent, ignorant, superstitious, jealous, cowardly, and more filthy and dirty than the imagination can conceive in dress and manner of living."

The officers were able to travel by dogsled to visit local Russian officials, who were generous with what few European delicacies they owned: butter, figs, honey, rice, and tea. The Russians found it astonishing that the ships had been gone so long and that so many were still alive.

King was among those who were deeply moved when a Russian showed him a pewter spoon marked with the word *London* on the back. He suddenly

Married Kamchadal women wore "hansome Silk Handkerchiefs bound round their heads," wrote King.

felt terribly homesick. It was their first chance to find out a few details about six-month-old news from Europe. Their hosts seemed to know almost nothing about the "American disturbance," only that war had been declared.

On June 15, the ships, still lingering in the harbor, experienced the explosion of Avachinskaya, a nearby volcano. Ashes and cinders about the size of peas covered the decks. The sky darkened. "The explosion was very loud at first," Ledyard wrote, "but gradually decreased until it subsided to a sound like that of a grumb[ling] distant thunder." The "awful appearance" and noise, followed by thunder and lightning, had a dampening effect on the superstitious men. Four days later, they were finally able to head out to sea and begin their northward journey again.

They were plagued by fog. By July 7, they had met with a huge drifting sheet of ice near Kotzebue Sound. For the next several days, in spite of hazy weather and snow, they tried to find some way past the ice to the north. Back and forth the ships tacked. Crew members had to lean out of the ship with long-handled hooks to try and shove away the biggest, sharpest pieces of ice.

Ledyard, like the others, was discouraged by this "fruitless search." "If a stranger was to see the countenances of the Inferior officers & men he would in compassion to them be," King said. "Such being the state of the ice, Capt Clerke, nor any one else, could see any prospect of getting any further to the Noward."

Their way was blocked by huge ice floes, covered with noisy walruses. Ice thumped against the bow and gouged the sheathing. For the next two weeks, the ships were battered with loose shards. They passed spouting whales and swimming polar bears.

Finally, on July 19, at latitude 70 degrees 33 minutes, five leagues short of Cook's last season a year earlier, Clerke admitted defeat. They would go no farther north. He gave orders to turn south when they saw the coast of Asia again.

Kamchadal villagers traveled with dog-drawn sledges on frozen rivers.

A month later, on August 22, thirty-eight-year-old Clerke died. He was buried with honors on shore at Paratonnka, a small village on the west side of Avacha Bay. The marines fired three volleys when his body was laid in the ground on August 29. Gore, Ledyard's friend, became the expedition leader and took command of the *Resolution*.

Chapter 17

HOMEWARD BOUND

From Avacha Bay to Cádiz, Spain
August 1779–October 1784

The brief arctic summer on the Siberian coast was in full bloom when the *Resolution* and *Discovery* arrived in late August 1779. The country was green. The men, who had just come from the ice, were staggered by so much lushness. "And the most agreeable Fragrancy I ever met with," Gilbert wrote. Ledyard and the other men spent time gathering firewood and water and brewing spruce beer. Carpenters worked on repairs to make ready for the homeward leg of the journey.

Gore consulted the other officers and came up with a plan to head for Japan, south around China, west around Africa, and back to England again.

"The summer here is of a very short duration being little more than four months," wrote Gilbert in October 1779, "for by October the Country began to have quite a wintry appearance." The trees lost their leaves. The grass turned gray. Ledyard and the others could sense that in less than a month, they would face snow. After seven weeks of increasingly bleak weather, they finally made preparations to set sail on the first week of October out of the bay around the southern extremity of Kamchatka.

Before they left, there was one last-minute romantic adventure. *Discovery* Marine Drummer Jeremiah Holloway delayed departure when he ran off October 9, 1779, with a Kamchadale sweetheart. A swelling in Holloway's

Kamchatka's brief summer transformed the dreary landscape surrounding the town of St. Peter and St. Paul.

knee had caused him severe lameness. A party of marines went to find him in the woman's home and brought him back to the ship.

The ships' delayed departure irritated many of the men, who were anxious to leave Kamchatka. The next day they finally left the bay with a dozen dogs and one of the Kamchadale sledges. The storms on the way around Japan "rendered our situation uncomfortable enough," wrote Samwell on November 25, 1779. Four days later, they dropped anchor in Macao, China, near the Canton River.

All of the journals, including Ledyard's, were confiscated and given to Gore to be kept in secrecy "with respect to our discoveries," Samwell wrote. The idea was to prevent anyone from publishing an account of the discoveries before Cook's journal could be edited. Ledyard, however, had other ideas.

Ledyard and the rest of the crew were delighted to finally hear definitive news from Europe—after an absence of nearly three years. For the first time, Ledyard learned what had happened when the American colonies rebelled against England. No end to the conflict was yet in sight.

The men got drunk on Chinese liquor called *sumchu*. They sold their Alaskan furs for outrageous prices. The Chinese bought small skins for seventy dollars each, furs which cost the sailors a hatchet or a saw to purchase from Indians. The prices were so unbelievable that two men, Quartermaster John

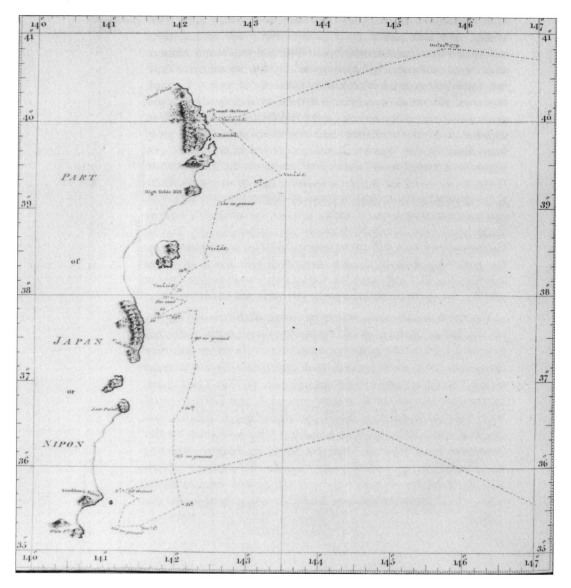

Captain John Gore charted a cautious course around the islands of Japan on their return voyage.

Cave and Seaman Michael Spencer, deserted. They stole the *Resolution*'s cutter and then vanished ashore into the Chinese crowd. They were certain of making huge profits selling furs in China, if they could only get back again to North America.

Cave and Spencer weren't the only ones impressed by the incredible profits to be made. Ledyard also wondered how he might be able to make some kind of fortune of his own in the fur trade. Perhaps the voyage wasn't such a failure after all.

Because of news of war between England and Spain, Ledyard and the other marines were put on special alert as the two ships crept around Africa past Table Bay. An extra cannon was purchased and special reinforcements were added to the ship's sides. The hapless marines practiced shooting off guns and managed to injure a carpenter's mate, who broke his arm. Another seaman named James Flood suffered severe burns.

Gore had received special letters of neutrality. This would help if the ships encountered the Spanish, but everyone knew there was no dissuading pirates. Gore did not wish to take any chances. After a "tedious stay of one month" in Cape Agulhas, South Africa, gathering supplies, they finally set sail for England. For three months, two weeks, and three days, they were completely out of sight of any land—a record for the voyage.

The wind and currents did not cooperate. They tried to return to England through the Channel and the River Thames but the eastern winds were against them. "We stood to the northward for the western coast of Ireland, with an intention to put into Galway," but that did not work either. For an entire week or ten days they beat off the coast, Gilbert said.

Finally, on August 21, 1780, they made the western islands of Scotland, which was the first land Ledyard had seen since they left Africa more than three months earlier. Although so close, they were still far from a safe harbor.

For some unstated reason, Gore refused to let the men go ashore for another entire month. Every delay made the rest of the crew doubt his skill. The sailors cursed Gore, "the only person in the fleet that does not eagerly wish to get home." By September 9, they were calling him "that old conceited American, who never conformed to any scheme of which he was not the proposer, who never took advice in his life," and "an indolent old man," wrote Trevenen. They felt cut off from the rest of the world, even though they were so close to family and friends. "We cou'd get no more intiligence concerning our Friends than if we had been at Otaheite," complained Gilbert.

On September 22, 1780, while the ships were lingering in the rocking waves off Scotland, Marine Sergeant Samuel Gibson died. He was Ledyard's superior. He had become ill off the Strait of Sunda, near Malay, described by one sailor as "one of the hottest and most unhealthy places in the world." Gibson recovered enough to go ashore on a brief leave and marry a local girl from Stromness. And then, quite suddenly, he died. He was buried in Scotland.

His death had a direct effect on Ledyard, who was made sergeant in his place. For Ledyard, this was something of a hollow victory. He had liked Gibson and there was no glory in this promotion, which had not been a reward for valor.

Ledyard enjoyed his new rank aboard ship for only two weeks. On September 30, the ships came to anchor at Yarmouth Roads to replace a new cable. They sailed up the Thames on October 7, 1780, and the *Discovery* tied up near a hulk at Woolwich. The *Resolution* went up to Deptford.

Unlike on earlier Cook expeditions, no cheering crowds awaited them. "Both ships were immediately clear'd," said Gilbert, "and their Crews paid their full wages, as a sixth rate, and set at liberty from the service except the marines who were sent to their division." After deductions for clothes, tobacco, and venereal treatment, Ledyard received exactly 27 pounds 16 shillings and 2½ pence for four years of work. He said good-bye to his friends and headed with the rest of the marines to a new post, 27th Company, Plymouth Division.

The harbor was filled with warships. Ledyard was a marked man. He was tan and lean and his hands were tattooed. He wore sailor's clothes and walked with a sailor's rolling gait. Press gangs, or teams of impressment officers, roamed the streets of harbor towns and captured anyone who looked like a sailor to work on British warships. England was still at war with America, so Ledyard couldn't go home.

Maybe he didn't want to return. Not yet. He was a sergeant now. In June

1781, eight months after he landed in England, Ledyard applied for a promotion. He used his contact with John Gore, who had been promoted to post captain at Greenwich Hospital, a luxurious position that meant steady pay and little work.

Gore forwarded Ledyard's letter to the Earl of Sandwich on June 21, 1781:

> I had the honour to sail with Captain Cook on his last Voyage upon Discoveries and though in quite a private station it is well known I merited much of his esteem and more than once have been entrusted with very honorable commands as will appear from his own Journals, nor was my conduct less acceptable to Capt. Clerke who succeeded him, and I am also happy to say that Capt. Gore who succeeded them both is equally disposed to represent to Your Lordship as a deserving Soldier. . . . May it please your Lordship, I understand that I am already on the list of those offered to your lordships consideration for promotion but as yet nothing in my favour has transpired . . . I am a native of North America, of a good Family and once had considerable connections there, untill the rupture with England in 1775 when I abandoned all and entered the Army here, where I flatter myself as I have been so I shall be encouraged. . . .

In his letter, Ledyard used "your Lordship" eleven times and claimed he had "abandoned all" in America.

Gore prefaced Ledyard's bit of begging with this introduction:

> Serjeant Ledyard is a Young active Man [who] hath done Good service on our late Circumnavigating Voyage, and Is one who from Education and abilities is (I think) Properly Qualified and justly merits a higher Rank Than That which he holds at present. My wish is to recommend him to your Lordships notice In hopes That by your means a Good Officer may not be Lost by being continued the Serjeant.

Gore's request fell on deaf ears. Lord Sandwich never made Ledyard's promotion, perhaps because he was pestered by so many people asking for similar favors. He once complained privately, "It really makes me tired of my situation. More is wanted than there is possibility of giving."

Ledyard decided to give up on the British Royal Marines. When his British ship docked at Long Island, New York, sometime in the early fall of 1782, he deserted.

He had been gone from home exactly seven years, the amount of time he had predicted in his 1774 letter to his cousin Isaac Ledyard: "I allot myself a seven years ramble more." His family was shocked to see him—a world traveler and celebrity. He had been with the famous Cook. He had journeyed around the world. His only possessions were a desk and a trunk with a few books, including *Tristam Shandy,* a popular novel by Laurence Sterne that would influence his own writing.

Disoriented and perplexed by his old surroundings, he wrote to Isaac, whom he called "Monecca," in January 1783:

> You will be surprized to hear of my being at Hartford—I am surprized myself. I made my escape from the British at Huntington Bay Long Island: went by virtue of a Permit of Seven Days liberty, which cost me the full sacrifice of Seven years hard service, to South Hold and from thence crossed the Sound. I am now at Mr. Seymours, and as happy as a bee. I have a little cash, Three pairs of Breeches, Three Waistcoats, Six pairs of Stockings, Two Coats and half a dozen ruffled shirts. I am a violent whig, and a violent Tory—Many are my acquaintenance, and not one out of the Pales of the family know me. I eat & drink when I am asked, and visit when I am invited: and in short generally do as I am bid. All I want of my Friends is Friendship; and possessed of that I am happy. . . .

He signed his letter with his pen name, Josephus.

He was as out of place back in staid Connecticut as Omai had been in London. No one quite understood what he'd done or what he'd seen. He seemed odder than ever, transformed into something that none of his relatives recognized: an adventurer who had circled the globe.

Of course, he enjoyed being petted and shown about town. He saw his mother, who was running an inn on Long Island. She was a widow and down on her luck. Living at home with her was a disabled grown son, a spinsterish daughter, and three more teenage girls. Ledyard had not brought back a fortune. He was of no help in his mother's economic struggle or his sisters' dowry support.

If anyone asked Ledyard the uncomfortable question about what he had done during the war, he cleverly avoided answering. America was its own country now. Many of his relatives and neighbors had died during the revolution, while he was busy serving the British in the Royal Marines. He didn't mention that unpleasantness, of course. Or the fact that he had applied for a promotion.

During the winter, between visits and socializing, he wrote his book—a new way to make himself famous. He holed up in his uncle Seymour's attic in Hartford during the winter of 1783 and began work on his travel writings. He had smuggled along a copy of *Discovery* Lieutenant John Rickman's book about the voyage, published in London in 1781—much to the dismay of Lord Sandwich. Cook's official version of the journey would not appear until 1784.

Since his notes had been confiscated in China, Ledyard went to work on his American version from memory. He had backing from a Connecticut bookseller and printer named Nathaniel Patten, who promised to pay him twenty guineas. Ledyard wrote rapidly. He was in such a hurry, he copied the last half of Rickman's book almost outright.

Ledyard's 208-page work had a very long title: *A Journal of Captain Cook's Last Voyage to the Pacific Ocean and in Quest of a North-West Passage, between Asia & America*. Americans were so eager to read the work, it was published in two parts. The first came out in June 1783, the second in July of the same year. The book was a best-seller, in spite of its errors.

Even before he finished the work, Ledyard lost interest in the book. As his cousin Isaac explained, "Being in haste to pursue his adventures, as soon as he had indulged his eager wishes to see his Friends, he allowed himself no time to compile and arrange the Papers, but left them with some person of that place [Hartford] in a loose and disordered state, of course they went in to an incorrect as well as a verry inelegent edition."

Ledyard was an undisciplined writer. Sitting at a desk with pen and paper for hours had little appeal to him. He was restless again, eager for travel. He decided to revive an old scheme and make his fortune on the furs he had seen in the Pacific Northwest.

In May 1783, he set off to try and raise capital he needed to go back to sea. His plan was to outfit a ship and crew and set up lucrative trade between the Pacific Northwest and China. He'd be rich in no time. His idea became, he said, his "hobby horse," a term he borrowed from *Tristam Shandy* that described something between an interest and an obsession.

Ledyard traveled to Philadelphia in May 1783 to look for investors. Instead he discovered what he told his cousin Isaac Ledyard was "the nakedness of things here." There seemed little possibility for "home navigation." The American economy after the revolution was in a shambles. He went to Boston, New London, and then New York.

Everywhere he went he encountered the same difficulty. No American merchant believed his story or felt comfortable with the risk. No one would back him in his enterprise. He was broke once again. His letters to his cousin were filled with the familiar refrain: "For God sake send me some money."

The following year he decided to abandon America and go to Spain, France—maybe even England—in search of investors. He said hasty farewells to his mother, sisters, and brothers. In August 1784, he landed in Cádiz, Spain, and became adept at playing the role of the exotic American among the gentry with "only half a Dollar & four Rials in my pocket." He became something of a charming quick-change artist living in "this Harlequin state of Existance."

In his letters to his cousin he described terrific happiness followed by fits of "uncommon melancholy." He was drinking too much. His health was poor. And still he had no investors—only more promises, more delays.

On October 12, 1784, he wrote to Isaac: "I am no otherwise the mad, romantic, dreaming Ledyard."

Chapter 18

A CHANCE MEETING

From Cádiz, Spain, to Cairo, Egypt
1784–1789

Paris was a vital, unpredictable city when Ledyard arrived in 1784. The cosmopolitan atmosphere—like no other in Europe or America—nurtured an extraordinary array of talented scientists, philosophers, artists, musicians, and writers. A construction boom had created new, impressive boulevards, grand open squares, and palatial public buildings.

But existing side by side with this grandeur were poverty, hunger, and governmental corruption. In 1784 murmurings of revolution—inspired by the American colonies' break with Britain—were first being heard in the back streets and alleys of Paris.

Ledyard was no stranger to the dark, destitute side of this glittering capital. His first two years there were, he said, "curiously wretched." Every attempt he made to find a financial backer for his Pacific fur trade company ended in failure. Poor, hungry, and mostly living on handouts, Ledyard stopped writing home. All that he would later reveal to his cousin Isaac about his early days in Paris was that his life was "villainous, unprofitable."

In February 1786, everything changed for Ledyard. He met forty-three-year-old Thomas Jefferson, the newly appointed American ambassador to France. How they met is not certain. "Without anything but a clean shirt," Ledyard bragged to Isaac Ledyard in a letter written that month, "was I invited from a gloomy garret to the splendid Tables of the first characters in this kingdom."

Lively, charming Americans living in Paris were considered fascinating dinnertime companions by French intellectuals, who had exalted ideas about democracy and republics. Some American expatriates, who formed their own close-knit community, were more than happy to take advantage of their status with amiable French hosts. Exotically tattooed Ledyard, as part of this community, had undoubtedly heard of the widely respected new ambassador from America. He was eager to meet Jefferson.

It's hard to imagine two more different men. Jefferson was everything Ledyard was not: methodical and self-controlled, with an obsessive determination to keep busy. (His motto was Virgil's saying, "Hard work overcomes everything.") Recently widowed, Jefferson had been beset by depression when he arrived alone in Paris in the gloomy, rainy fall of 1784. He was homesick for his family and his beloved Virginia. By 1786, he was becoming more accustomed to his new urban life. And he had made remarkable progress navigating the perilous, corrupt French court.

What attracted Jefferson to Ledyard most certainly was conversation. They were both great talkers, who delighted in discourse that was "loose and rambling," as one contemporary noted. Like Ledyard, Jefferson enjoyed scattering information "wherever he went."

There was so much to talk about. News of enormous, mysterious animal bones recently uncovered in America. The customs of North American Indians. The joys of French theater. Theories on magnetism and the connection between Asian and North American native peoples. Of course, Ledyard enjoyed nothing more than regaling Jefferson with his adventures in exotic, distant places—Tahiti, Hawaii, Alaska, Siberia. Ledyard shared a copy of his book about Cook's expedition. Jefferson found it fascinating.

Throughout the spring and summer of 1786, they talked late into the night over dinners prepared by Jefferson's cook, with fine wines from the ambassador's famous wine cellar. They talked as they rambled through the streets of Paris, buying books along the quay and purchasing an expensive pair of

Thomas Jefferson is portrayed in an engraving based on a portrait created by Rembrandt Peale in 1801, after Jefferson became president.

pumps from a cobbler shop. Jefferson, a slender man with graying red hair, strolled with "a loose, shackling air." His chiseled face looked intent as he listened to animated Ledyard.

At age thirty-five, Ledyard, who described himself as "plump and hearty & merry as a fool," was no longer a young man. He was canny enough to know that enthusiastic Jefferson and his Parisian contacts might provide his last chance to launch his venture. In February 1786, he revealed to Jefferson his burning desire to "make some discoveries which will benefit society and insure [me] a small degree of honest fame."

Ledyard had a genuine admiration for Jefferson, a quiet, reserved man who nonetheless shared Ledyard's optimism and eclectic interests. Ledyard called Jefferson "my brother my father my friend." Likewise, Jefferson found Ledyard a fascinating, singular individual. He was impressed with Ledyard's "genius, and education better than common, and a talent for useful and interesting information." Ledyard seemed to Jefferson, who was never a completely astute judge of character, to be "an honest man, and a man of truth." (In fact, by the end of the summer, Jefferson had lent Ledyard 276 francs, for which he was never repaid.)

Ledyard's spirit of enterprise made a big impression on Jefferson the ambassador. He was especially fascinated by Ledyard's fantastic stories about the rich resources and fur trade in the Pacific Northwest—information backed up by subsequent accounts published about Cook's last voyage. Part of Jefferson's job in Paris was to cobble together trade agreements to help the struggling, fledgling American economy, which had been crippled by the war with Britain. The possibility of unlimited wealth and resources in the mostly vacant lands of western North America tantalized Jefferson.

Even though this vast region was still officially owned by France, Spain, and Russia, farsighted Jefferson had considered westward expansion as early as 1785. He envisioned an "empire of liberty" stretching all the way to the West Coast. The economic possibilities seemed unlimited.

Eager for facts, figures, and details about the West, Jefferson responded enthusiastically when Ledyard told him about his daring, wild plan to undertake a solo journey through the northern parts of Asia and America. Encouraging Ledyard to make such an amazing, dangerous trip might ultimately be helpful to the struggling American nation. On February 9, 1786, Jefferson wrote a hasty, excited note to tell his friend the Marquis de Lafayette about Ledyard's scheme. "Should he get safe through it," Jefferson wrote, "I think he will give an interesting account of what he shall have seen."

Jefferson's eager interest was all Ledyard needed. He was fired once again with determination. "Let a native [of the North American continent] explore its Boundary," he declared to his cousin on August 8, 1786. "It is my wish to be that man."

After spending the next three months unsuccessfully trying to find a ship that would take him from Europe to Nootka Sound, on what is now Vancouver Island, Canada, Ledyard decided to follow Jefferson's advice and cross Asia overland to Kamchatka and then from there locate passage by sea to North America, where he would begin his eastward trek through unknown wilderness. He impatiently decided to go ahead with this scheme before he received official papers from the Russian government to cross the country.

On November 25, 1786, he wrote to Jefferson from London with excitement:

> I am indeed a very plain man, but do not think that mountains or oceans shall oppose my passage to glory while I have such friends in remembrance—I have pledged myself—difficulties have intervened—my heart is on fire. . . . I still am persecuted—still the slave of accident and son of care.

In the same letter, he hinted at a growing problem with his temper. While attending a play in London, he was insulted by a few theatergoers, perhaps something to do with being an American. Ledyard bragged to Jefferson that as a result, he was "obliged to thrash five or six of these haughty turbulent and very insolent people."

He left London in December 1786 and arrived in Germany, where he bought two large dogs, an Indian pipe, and a hatchet—his only supplies. He was again delayed. His dogs died. He managed finally to get to Hamburg.

He departed in the dead of winter in January 1787 and traveled up through snowy Denmark, Sweden, Lapland, and Finland and then south again to St. Petersburg—covering 1,200 miles in eight weeks, an amazing feat. He walked and hitchhiked rides on sleighs and made twenty miles a day. He survived mostly through the hospitality of the few people he met on the way. (He was always impressed with the generosity of women.) He spoke French to "wolves,

Panoramic view of St. Petersburg as it may have appeared to Ledyard on his ill-fated Russian journey in 1787. This etching was made from a sketch by J. A. Atkinson and was published in 1805.

rocks, woods and snow" to keep himself sane as he traveled alone through empty, hostile country.

His fortune changed in November 1787, when he reached Yakutsk, nearly three thousand miles from St. Petersburg. By chance he met with Joseph Billings, a former sailor on the *Discovery*. Ledyard thought this was his lucky break. Billings was commanding a Russian expedition to explore the Bering Sea and said that Ledyard could come along as a passenger. Billings invited Ledyard to go with him east to Irkutsk, where he planned to pick up supplies for his expedition.

Unfortunately, Billings may have had treachery on his mind. On January 17, 1788, Ledyard was arrested as a spy by the Russian government and dragged back to St. Petersburg in a brutal sledge and pony express that traveled one thousand miles of the journey nearly nonstop in a week. Clearly, the

This is the same kind of horse-drawn sledge that carried Ledyard at breakneck speed from Siberia to St. Petersburg after he was arrested as a spy.

Russians did not like the idea of any Americans muscling in on the Pacific Northwest fur trade, which they considered their monopoly. Ledyard was eventually booted across the Polish border. "Go back to England," his guards told him.

In early May 1788, using borrowed money, he stumbled back to London with his Siberian journal, a grubby reindeer-skin coat, boots, and socks, a Siberian red fox cap, fox-skin gloves, and not much else. His health ruined, the emaciated thirty-seven-year-old was warmly received by Sir Joseph Banks, president of the Royal Society and former scientist on Cook's second voyage.

Banks invited Ledyard to take part in a new expedition: tracing the course of the River Niger and locating the fabled city of Timbuktu in "deepest

Africa." The Association for Promoting the Discovery of the Interior Parts of Africa was delighted to have him as a volunteer.

When the association representatives asked him when he'd be ready to leave, Ledyard replied, "Tomorrow morning."

Before leaving London, in June 1788, he penned a few revealing words in his hasty, dramatic scrawl. First he informed his mother, who had not seen him since 1784, that he was going to Africa and would be gone for another three years. "Behold me the greatest traveller in history exccentric, irregular, rapid, unaccountable, curious and without vanity, majestic as a comet. I afford a new character to the world, and a new subject to biography." His words to her were so full of wild boasting, they seemed to hint that he knew he was never coming back.

Ledyard's parting gesture to his beloved cousin Isaac was to send him his unfinished portrait, which had been painted by a deaf-mute artist in Sweden on his Russia trip. Ledyard claimed a friend called it "a perfect likeness," then added that he thought the picture had become a "Shadow of Josephus." He sent another, smaller, copy to his mother, saying, "It is the only thing I ever presented to the dear Woman."

Ledyard may have been too embarrassed at first to see Jefferson in person when he arrived in Paris on his way to Africa. He penned a brief note to be delivered to Jefferson's hotel on July 4, 1788. He claimed to be ill with a cold. He may have been trying to avoid Jefferson's displeasure when he found out that Ledyard had signed up with an expedition designed to benefit the British. "He is now on his way to Africa," Ledyard's cryptic note to Jefferson said, "to see what he can do with that continent."

During his week in Paris, Ledyard eventually saw Jefferson before he proceeded to Marseilles and caught a ship sailing for Alexandria. He reached Alexandria on August 15. His plan was to join a caravan of camels and traders leaving for Sennar, a city in present-day Sudan. On November 15, 1788, after numerous delays in Cairo, what he called "a wretched hole," he wrote what would be his last letter to Jefferson, which ended with: "Indeed it would be a consolation to think of you in my last moments. Be happy."

In January 1789, Ledyard was still in Cairo, waiting for a caravan's arrival to take him into the interior. One day, he could stand the delays no longer. Thirty-eight-year-old Ledyard flew into such a rage, "he deranged something in his system." To cure his terrible stomachache, he took a powerful emetic. The overdose caused his death.

He died alone—without family or friends nearby. His grave in the desert was unmarked. No one who had been close to him heard of his death for nearly half a year.

EPILOGUE

Not until May 21, 1789, when hawthorn trees bloomed and bloody riots had spilled out onto the streets of Paris, did Thomas Jefferson hear of Ledyard's death in Africa. At first he refused to believe it. How could someone who had survived Siberian winters, tropical hurricanes, Hawaiian warrior attacks, and arctic high seas simply vanish—never to return?

For Jefferson, the news was tragic. He had lost not only a fellow countryman who had energy and promise, but he had also lost a friend.

It seemed that Ledyard had made Jefferson a promise in private conversation in Paris before he left for Africa. Ledyard had never entirely given up on his dream to explore North America. If he returned alive from Africa, he had vowed to "go to Kentuckey," Jefferson wrote sadly in a letter to James Madison, "and endeavor to penetrate Westwardly from thence to the South Seas."

Although Ledyard never made the transcontinental trek he imagined, his wild, daring notion had a lasting impact on Jefferson. Ultimately, Jefferson's perseverance and support made it possible for an expedition to successfully "endeavor to penetrate Westwardly."

It would take Jefferson two more tries over the next fifteen years to find an expedition with the proper financial backing and expertise to make the journey to the Pacific.

In 1792, Jefferson proposed to the American Philosophical Society to send French botanist André Michaux up the Missouri River and across the Rockies to the Pacific. When the French government heard about this idea, they angrily called Michaux back.

In January 1803, the Louisiana Purchase became a reality. Now as third president of the United States, Jefferson insisted that the West should be

Etching from original Journal of the Voyages and Travels of a Corps of Discovery, *showing Lewis and Clark holding a council with Indians*

explored for the sake of the fur trade and, even more important, to gather scientific information. The Lewis and Clark Expedition, led by Captain Meriwether Lewis and William Clark, received funding from Congress and personal backing from President Jefferson.

In 1804, the expedition set off on an amazing journey—a kind of mobile scientific laboratory. On their 4,134-mile outward journey, they traveled from St. Louis, up the Missouri River, across the plains, through the Rockies, and finally down the Columbia River. By foot, riverboat, canoe, and horseback, they collected information about climate, weather, plants, animals, minerals, rivers, mountains, and Indians.

Finally, on the wet, disagreeable afternoon of November 7, 1805, the expedition arrived almost in sight of the Pacific. In spite of the bad weather, they were "all cheerful and full of anxiety to see further into the ocean," Clark wrote.

Present-day Astoria, Oregon, is only 120 miles north of the spot where the *Resolution* first sighted New Albion's coast in 1778. On a rainy overlook near Astoria twenty-seven years later stood Lewis and Clark. They gazed out at the stormy Pacific. In spirit, if not in body, Ledyard was with them.

Appendix A

Ships' Companies
(Those Who Make an Appearance in *Magnificent Voyage*)

DISCOVERY

Captain Charles Clerke (1743–1779), commander of the *Discovery*, was thirty-two when the voyage began—his third expedition with Cook. He was Cook's highest-ranking officer. The *Discovery* was delayed in leaving England because Clerke was still in English debtors' prison, where he was serving a sentence for signing his name to his brother's bad debt. Cook, who did not know Clerke was in jail, left word that he must meet the *Resolution* at Table Bay in South Africa. Little did anyone realize that generous, amiable Clerke had contracted a fatal disease, tuberculosis, while in the filthy, damp prison.

First Lieutenant James "Jem" Burney (1750–1821) served directly under Clerke. He first went to sea as a captain's servant when he was ten years old. From a wealthy family, the twenty-six-year-old was fluent in Tahitian and had musical ability. He was promoted to captain in 1782 and fought the French in the West Indies. He eventually retired as a rear admiral.

Master Thomas Edgar kept a journal about his experiences on the voyage. When he returned to England, he was promoted to lieutenant; sadly, he developed an extreme drinking problem.

Second Lieutenant John Rickman wrote an anonymous account of the voyage; Ledyard drew on it to write his own version of the journey.

Surgeon John Law assisted with medical work.

Midshipman George Vancouver (1757–1798), the nineteen-year-old "young gentleman," had sailed with Cook on his second voyage. He joined Ledyard on his Mauna Loa trip. When he returned to England, he received appointment as a lieutenant. He served in the West Indies and later sailed to the northwest coast of North America, where, from 1792 to 1794, he expertly charted Puget Sound, the mouth of the Columbia River, and stretches of the California and Alaska coastlines.

Gunner's Mate Simeon Woodruff, American born, eventually returned to Connecticut.

Astronomer William Bayly (1737–1810) was the son of an English farmer. Much like Cook, he displayed unusual mathematic aptitude as a boy. He served as astronomer's assistant on Cook's second voyage. When he returned home from the third voyage, he became headmaster of the Royal Naval Academy at Portsmouth.

Botanist David Nelson, a Kew gardener, was originally hired by Sir Joseph Banks to collect specimens for his private collection.

Able Seaman Joseph Billings, age eighteen, assisted the astronomer, Bayly. He later joined the Russian navy and was appointed to command a nine-year expedition to explore northeastern parts of Asia and the Bering Sea. By chance, he met Ledyard in eastern Siberia.

Quartermaster William Hollamby, thirty-year-old Londoner who worked his way up from able seaman to master's mate by the end of the journey, later became a lieutenant and a commander.

Gunner's Mate Thomas Shaw tried to desert at Raiatea in November 1779.

Midshipman Alexander Mouat joined Shaw in unsuccessful desertion at Raiatea and was severely punished. He later became a commander.

Able Seaman and Servant John McIntosh was nineteen when he began the voyage. The young Scotsman was killed when he was hurled down the hatchway in a storm in October 1778.

Able Seaman James Flood was injured on homeward passage in June 1780.

Complete List of Royal Marines

Sergeant James Kich fell overboard but was rescued.

Corporal George Harrison drowned en route to Table Bay, Africa.

Privates:

William Broom

William Brown deserted at the Cape of Good Hope.

John Herriott

Jeremiah Holloway, drummer, attempted to desert when he fell in love with a Kamchadale woman.

Christopher Kerwin

George Moody, drowned

Michael Newman
James Poole
William Randall became corporal when Harrison died.
Hamlet Thompson

RESOLUTION

Captain James Cook (1728–1779) was commander of the expedition. At six feet two inches, Cook towered over most of his crew. (The average height for grown men at the time was five feet six inches.) Cook was large-boned and had a powerful build. His features were strongly marked: high forehead, large nose, prominent eyebrows, and determined mouth. One officer described Cook's face as "full of expression," good-looking in a plain sort of way. He wore his brown hair long, pulled back in a queue, or what we would call a ponytail. He was hardy and athletic, yet he never learned to swim.

His hands were large, his palms broad. If Ledyard or the other crew members looked closely at Cook's right hand, they would have noticed a curious scar that ran between his forefinger and thumb all the way to his wrist. This scar was the result of a gunpowder explosion in 1764 that nearly cost Cook his life while he was making maps off the Newfoundland coast. A month later he was back at work again—bandage or no. He was a driven, ambitious man who took his professional responsibilities seriously.

James Cook had humble beginnings. He was born on October 27, 1728, in the village of Marton-in-Cleveland in a two-room clay biggin, or cottage, on the moors of northern England. He was the second son of a Yorkshire farm laborer who never owned his own land. As a child, Cook's eagerness to learn and his obviously bright mind encouraged his father's employer to pay for Cook's schooling. When he became a teenager, he sidestepped a possible career as a shopkeeper and went to sea. After being apprenticed to a coal shipper in Whitby, North Yorkshire, Cook had his training in the perilous North Sea.

When a series of navy skirmishes in 1755 launched the Seven Years War in Europe, Cook left the secure but dull coal trade and volunteered as an able seaman in the navy. This was a dangerous, low-paying job, but it offered the possibility of advancement if Cook survived. He proved himself capable, and was quickly promoted to master's mate. He enthusiastically learned surveying, or map making. His accomplished charting skills landed him a job mapping the St. Lawrence River. His detailed charts made his reputation as a respected surveyor.

Cook had the good fortune to serve under officers who were willing to teach him higher levels of mathematics and astronomy—two of Cook's favorite subjects. In 1766 he observed an eclipse of the sun and sent his results to the Royal Society. Members of the scientific organization were impressed.

The Royal Society, with backing from the king, had been planning an expedition to the South Pacific to chart an eclipse of the sun. Scientists at the time believed that this phenomenon, called the transit of Venus, would help them calculate the dimensions of the universe. Such an opportunity would not come again for another hundred years.

At the last moment the scientist who was supposed to head the expedition was barred by the Admiralty from assuming sole command of a navy vessel. Cook's luck again proved critical. In 1768 forty-year-old Cook was promoted from master to lieutenant and assumed command of the *Endeavour,* a kind of floating, fully equipped scientific laboratory.

On Cook's first round-the-world expedition (1768–1771), the transit of Venus was successfully recorded. More than five thousand miles of unexplored coastline were charted. Cook mapped Tahiti, the Society Islands, and most of New Zealand; and he claimed all of Australia for England.

His reputation secure, on his return Cook was rewarded with another promotion and a second voyage (1772–1775), this time with two ships. On the seventy-thousand-mile expedition, he proved once and for all that there was no such thing as "the Great Southern Continent," which European geographers had believed existed somewhere in the South Pacific. Cook also explored and claimed for England lands that are now known as Easter Island, New Hebrides, New Caledonia, and Norfolk Island.

After he sailed closer to the South Pole than anyone had before, Cook confided revealingly in a letter to a friend: "ambition leads me not only farther than any other man has before me, but as far as I think it possible for a man to go."

Left behind after Cook's death in 1779 was his widow, Elizabeth Batts Cook. They had married in 1762. During the seventeen years of their marriage, Cook had been home a total of only three years. Of the six children Elizabeth bore, three died before age four. Cook was at sea during the births, deaths, and burials of all except one.

Among Captain James Cook's survivors were his eldest son, also named James, who became a naval officer and was killed in a robbery attempt in 1794. Another son, Nathaniel, also went to sea. Unfortunately, he died in a shipwreck a year after his father's murder. The youngest son, Hugh (named after Cook's patron, Lord Hugh Palliser), had been born in May 1776, only a few months before Cook left on his last voyage. Hugh, who hoped to become a minister, died from a fever in 1793 at age seventeen.

Elizabeth became a childless widow, and lived to be ninety-three. She remained devoted to her famous husband's memory. She wore a lock of his hair in her ring—the custom of the time. In old age, if anyone said or did anything improper in her presence, her favorite comment was "Mr. Cook would never have done so."

First Lieutenant John Gore (c. 1730–1790), born in Virginia, was both a respected officer and friend to Ledyard. If anything happened to Clerke, Gore was next in line of command. Although only in his late thirties, Gore was the oldest officer on the voyage other than Cook. Fair-skinned with thinning red hair, he was described by his shipmates as cheerful and optimistic. He was an experienced Pacific sailor who had already been around the world three times. An accomplished marksman, Gore enjoyed shooting kangaroo on Cook's earlier voyage to Australia. His hunting skills came in handy whenever the ship landed and fresh meat was needed. After the voyage, he never went to sea again. He was appointed post captain of Greenwich Hospital, the position Cook had given up to lead the third expedition.

Next in the line of command was *Second Lieutenant James King* (1750–1784), only a year older than Ledyard. The son of an English parson, King had entered the navy at age twelve and later went on to study science in college. His navy background had given him skills as an amateur astronomer and as a perceptive observer of new cultures, both of which proved useful on Cook's third voyage. A refined intellectual, King was described by a midshipman as "one of the politest, genteelest and best bred men." After the death of Clerke, he took over command of the *Discovery*. When he returned to England, he was promoted to captain and was given command of a five-hundred-ship convoy to the West Indies. Unfortunately, the voyage ruined his health.

Irish-born *Third Lieutenant John Williamson* was anything but polite and genteel. Of all the men aboard the *Resolution,* he was one of the most unpopular. He had a bad temper and a self-righteous streak. When he returned, he rose to command a ship during the Battle of Camperdown, in 1797, but was court-martialed for unbecoming conduct and prohibited from ever serving on a Royal Navy ship.

The *Resolution*'s master was *William Bligh* (1754–1817), born in Devon, England, and just twenty-two years old. As master, it was his responsibility to keep careful records in the ship's log and chart all soundings and the ship's general navigation. He was also a kind of general manager on the ship, making sure the masts, yards, sails, rigging, and stores were in proper condition at all times. Unfortunately, Bligh was vain and quick to insult. Of medium height with a sharp nose, thin mouth, and close-set blue eyes, Bligh was "prone to see fools about him too easily." (This trait would get him into mutinous trouble later in life.) Although a rather intense young man, Bligh was an excellent navigator and mapmaker.

When he returned, he became famous for two mutinies, one on the *Bounty*, in 1789, and another in New South Wales, in 1808. His navigational skills saved his life: he managed to direct a small boat containing himself and several other castaway sailors from the *Bounty* several thousand miles over open seas to safety.

Surgeon William Anderson (1748–1778) was a young Scotsman who was interested in natural history and had a good ear for learning new languages. He brought along his own scientific equipment. This was his second voyage with Cook. Described as pleasant and generous, Anderson, like Clerke, was unknowingly infected with tuberculosis before the expedition began.

Surgeon's First Mate David Samwell (c. 1751–1799) acted as Anderson's assistant. This son of a Welsh minister was something of a poet and a lady's man. He later became a writer for *Biographia Britannica* and wrote an honest account of Cook's death, which he added to an article, "Observations Respecting the Introduction of the Venereal Disease into the Sandwich Islands."

John Webber (c. 1750–1793), twenty-four years old, was the son of a Swiss sculptor. Before photography was invented, professional painters like Webber recorded people, places, plants, and animals in oil and charcoal sketches. Webber was educated in Paris. He worked rapidly and was considered a very valuable addition to the expedition. When he returned, he published a series of sixteen views of places visited on the voyage. He later became a regular exhibitor and full-fledged member of the prestigious Royal Academy.

Midshipman George Gilbert, eighteen when the voyage left, kept a journal about his experiences.

Midshipman James Trevenen (1760–1790), age sixteen, was the youngest "young gentleman" on board. After the voyage, he served as lieutenant in the West Indies with King. He later took a job as captain in the Russian navy and died in action against Sweden. He wrote his own account of Cook's last voyage.

Midshipman John Watts, another young gentleman.

Gunner Robert Anderson was a thirty-five-year-old Scotsman who joined Ledyard on the Mauna Loa exploration. This was his third voyage with Cook.

Able Seaman William Watman, age forty-four, was the oldest sailor on the *Resolution*. He had sailed three times with Cook. He died in Hawaii. "Belov'd by his fellows, for his good, & benevolent disposition," wrote King.

Able Seaman John Cave, age thirty, deserted on Macao. This was his second voyage with Cook.

Able Seaman Michael Spencer, age nineteen, also deserted on Macao.

Omai, a native of Tahiti, in the Society Islands, had been taken back to England on Cook's second voyage. His outward "good breeding," which pleased English society so much, vanished when he returned to his home islands. After a life of dissipation, he died sometime around 1789. His house and most of his possessions were destroyed by local natives. His two assistants, Tiarooa and Coaa, were said to have died around the same time of "homesickness." Forty years later, Omai's jack-in-the-box toy was still proudly owned by a Huahine chief.

Quartermaster Thomas Roberts from Bermuda died at sea of dropsy off Niihau, Hawaii, in January 1778.

Able Seaman John Grant eventually was promoted to quartermaster. In Kauai in March 1779 he refused to get in the escaping boat as a point of honor.

Carpenter's Mate Alexander McIntosh was described by King as "a very hard working quiet man." He died May 1779 in Petropavlovsk.

Complete List of Royal Marines

The officer in charge of the marines on board the *Resolution* was *Second Lieutenant Molesworth Phillips* (c. 1755–1832), a handsome young man with an interest in music. The *Resolution* and the *Discovery* each had its own set of marines to act as military guards and armed protection whenever needed. Phillips had a good military record, although there were those aboard who soon accused him of being lazy—"a bone idle fellow" who did not worry much about marine discipline. Bligh complained that Phillips "never did anything but eat and sleep." When he returned to England, he entered into a disastrous marriage with the sister of his fellow officer James Burney. He hobnobbed with wealthy society and retired a colonel. When he died in 1832 at age seventy-five, he was the longest-lived survivor of Cook's last voyage.

Under Phillips' command was *Sergeant Samuel Gibson*, who directly oversaw Ledyard and another corporal, fifteen privates, and a drummer. Gibson had originally shipped as a private on Cook's first voyage, in 1768. While in Tahiti during this expedition, he fell in love with a native girl, jumped ship, and ran away with her into the mountains. He was captured and punished, but reinstated by Cook. The adventure had one good result: Gibson became fluent in Tahitian. He enlisted on Cook's second voyage and was promoted to corporal of the marines. During this expedition, he was said to have saved Cook during a clash with Maori natives. Cook was fond of Gibson, his former deserter, and the marine sergeant hero-worshiped his commander.

Corporal James Thomas was killed at Kealakekua Bay.

Corporal John Ledyard

Privates:

John Allen was killed at Kealakekua Bay.

Richard Brown

Isaac Carley

Thomas Fatchett was also killed at Kealakekua Bay.

Thomas Girley

Thomas Harford

John Harrison fell in love with a native woman and tried to desert at Bora Bora.

Theophilus Hinks was killed at Kealakekua Bay.

John Jackson was wounded in the eye at Kealakekua Bay.

John James

John McDonald

John McLeod

Thomas Morris was punished for letting a prisoner escape at Huahine.

John Perkins

Michael Portsmouth, drummer

William Scruse

APPENDIX B

Time Line

November 1751	John Ledyard born in Groton, Connecticut Colony.
1753	Captain Ledyard has a near-wreck at sea.
	John Ledyard's brother George is born.
1754	Fanny, a sister, born.
1756	Thomas, a second brother, born disabled.
1757	Captain Ledyard's ship, the *Greyhound,* is hijacked; he retrieves the ship but not its cargo.
1762	Captain Ledyard dies.
	John Ledyard's uncle, father of Isaac and Benjamin, dies.
	John and family go to live in Southold, New York, with his mother's relatives.
1765	John Ledyard's mother remarries.
	John and his cousins Benjamin and Isaac go to live with their grandfather in Hartford, Connecticut.
1766	Explosion in Hartford kills Nathaniel Ledyard and five others.
1767	John Ledyard's half sister Abigail is born.
1769	John Ledyard's half sister Phoebe is born.
1770	John Ledyard's half sister Julia is born.
1771	John Ledyard's grandfather dies; John inherits almost nothing.
1772	Ledyard goes to Dartmouth; spends four months visiting Iroquois.
1773	Ledyard escapes Dartmouth in canoe downriver and returns to Hartford.
	Leaves America in a merchant ship.

1774	Jumps ship; joins British army; is brought back by captain.
1775	Goes to England to look for rumored rich relatives; doesn't find any.
1776	Signs up with 24th Company, Royal Marines, Plymouth Division, and sails on Cook's third voyage. His stepfather dies, leaving the family penniless. Mother, with six children, turns her house into a tavern.
August 1778	Ledyard treated for venereal disease.
October 1778	On a solo expedition into the interior, Ledyard meets Russian fur traders at Unalaska Island.
February 1779	Cook killed by Hawaiians at Kealakekua Bay.
September 1780	Ledyard promoted to sergeant after Gibson dies. The *Resolution* and the *Discovery* return to England.
October 1780	Ledyard paid off after paying for clothing, venereal disease treatment, and tobacco.
November 1780	Transfers to 27th Company, Plymouth Division.
June 1781	Through his friend John Gore, Ledyard applies to Lord Sandwich for a promotion; Sandwich never responds.
September 1781	In a massacre at Groton, Connecticut, near Fort Griswold, the British army kills many Ledyard family members and neighbors.
October 1781	British commander Cornwallis surrenders; the war between America and Britain officially ends. Rickman's version of Cook's third voyage is published in London.
Fall 1782	Ledyard deserts while his British ship is anchored near Long Island, forfeiting six years' service and risking court-martial. Goes to see his mother at her tavern.
1783	Rickman's book published in the United States.
Winter 1783	Ledyard writes his own version of the voyage.

Summer 1783	Ledyard's book is published and becomes a best-seller.
May 1783	Ledyard develops a scheme to set up trade between the American West Coast and Siberia.
	Goes to Philadelphia to attempt to find investors.
1784	First "official" version of Cook's voyage appears.
	Sails for Cádiz, Spain, and then travels on to France to find investors.
February 1786	Meets and befriends Thomas Jefferson, U.S. minister to France; Jefferson begins to negotiate for Ledyard's passage through Russia.
August 1786	Ledyard tries to find a ship to take him from England to what is now Vancouver, Canada, but fails.
December 1786	Sets out from London for Siberia overland, with two dogs; both die.
Winter 1786 to 1787	Ledyard walks from Stockholm, Sweden, around the Gulf of Bothnia to St. Petersburg, Russia. Arrives in St. Petersburg in March.
June 1787	Departs St. Petersburg for Siberia.
September 1787	Arrives in Irkutsk, having hiked, hitched rides, and canoed across Siberia.
January 1788	Arrested in Irkutsk as a spy.
March 1788	Deported across Russian border to Poland.
May 1788	Returns to London.
June 1788	Leaves London to explore Niger River in Africa.
January 1789	Dies in Cairo, Egypt.

Glossary

the Admiralty   executive department with authority over British naval affairs.

"All hands!"   whole ship's company, "Entire crew! Everybody!"

ballast   quantity of iron, stone, gravel, or other heavy substance placed in the lower hold of a ship to increase stability by lowering the center of gravity.

barometer   instrument that measures the pressure of the atmosphere. In most cases, when the air pressure changes, the weather will soon change as well.

bilge   (often pronounced "bill′idge") the lowest part of the interior of a boat, where water tends to collect ("bilge water").

boatswain   ("bo′sun") the officer in charge of sails, rigging, anchors, and cables. He also assembles the crew whenever they're required for duty and oversees the day-to-day work of the ship. A responsible position that requires action and thorough seaman's knowledge.

bow   forward part of the ship.

bowsprit   spar, or pole, that projects forward from the front of a ship and extends over the water. Connected to the bowsprit are stays for the rigging of jibs, small triangular sails that help increase a ship's efficiency. The bowsprit also balances supports for the ship's foremast and mainmast.

"Brace the yards sharp up!"   "Pull on the ropes connected to the booms, or yardarms, to trim the sails!" In other words, "Adjust the sails quickly so that the ship will move at her best!"

capstan   drum-shaped device in the front of the ship that can be used to raise the heavy anchor. Capstan bars are inserted into holes at the top of the capstan. The crew pushes these by hand. As the capstan moves, the chain connected to the anchor is shortened and the anchor rises out of the water.

chronometer   accurate clock used to calculate longitude, which helps determine a ship's position.

colliers   ships used to carry coal or ore.

cooper   one who makes or repairs wooden barrels.

cordage   the ropes in a ship's rigging.

cutter   small one-masted sailboat usually rigged with a mainsail and two jibs.

fathom   six feet.

flagship   the ship that carries the commander.

foremast   the mast closest to the bow, or front, of a ship.

foretops   sails set on the foremast, the mast closest to the bow.

gunner's mate   crew member who assists with the ship's guns and artillery.

"Hard astarboard!"   "Turn the ship to the right!" The starboard is the right side of the vessel, as viewed when facing the bow, or front.

heel   to incline or stoop to one side.

hogsheads   barrel-like containers that can hold up to sixty-three gallons.

hull   the main structure of a vessel, not including the deck, keel, or mast.

Jack Tar   a sailor in the Royal Navy, also called "tar."

main mast   the principal, tallest mast.

main topgallant   (pronounced "main t'garn") ring of rope placed around a spar for the purpose of moving it and adjusting a topmast.

main topmast   the second section of the mainmast.

mast   vertical pole that carries a ship's sails. Each section (from lowest to highest) has its own name: lower mast, topmast, topgallant mast, and royal mast. The *Resolution* was fitted with three masts: the foremast, at the bow, or front, of the ship; the mainmast, the tallest mast, in the middle; and the mizzenmast in the stern, or most toward the back of the ship. Each mast had to bear the weight of several heavy canvas sails, attached to long horizontal wooden poles called yards, and controlled by ropes, or rigging.

master   an officer who holds special certificates in navigation and seamanship.

mate   petty officer under the captain who helps the master. Also used to refer in general to an officer's assistant.

midshipmen   young gentlemen, often from wealthy families, who serve as apprentices with hopes of eventually becoming commissioned officers.

mizzenmast   the mast at the stern, or back, of a ship.

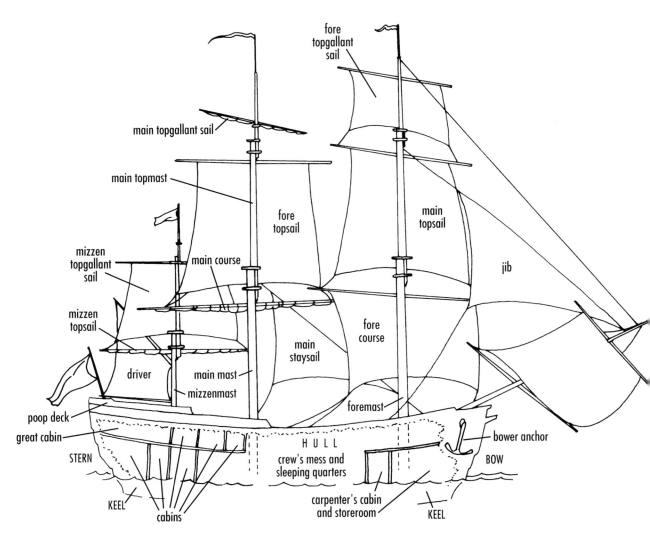

A full-rigged ship

mizzen topmast   the second section of the mizzenmast.

nautical mile   a unit of distance used at sea, taking into account the curvature of the earth; roughly equivalent to 6,067.12 feet or 1,852 meters. (A statute mile, used to measure distance on land, is equivalent to 5,280 feet.)

people   everyone on ship who isn't an officer; the general mass of sailors who take orders and perform hard labor.

pinnace   heavy, large rowing boat that can also be rigged with a sail.

planking   the wooden covering of the ribs of the hull; the ship's "skin."

poop deck   the raised deck at the stern, or back, of a ship.

port side   the left side of a boat as viewed when facing the bow, or front, of the boat.

privateers   ships that may officially have a special letter of marque, or commission, from their government to prey on an enemy's commerce for private gain. Often privateers operate without official commissions and are backed by private merchants.

quartermaster   crew member who steers the ship and is in charge of the navigating equipment.

rigging   ropes of a ship. Ropes used in hoisting, lowering, or setting sails are called running rigging. Ropes used to support masts, yards, and the bowsprit are called standing rigging.

scuttle   small glass-covered hatch, or opening, in the side of a ship to admit light and air.

sentinel   guard.

sextant   navigational instrument used to measure the vertical position of an object such as the sun, moon, or stars to determine a ship's position.

sheathing   covering of copper sheets on the bottom of a ship to protect the wood from marine borers, sea worms that eat holes in wood.

starboard   ("star'berd") the right side of a boat as viewed when facing the bow, or front, of the boat.

staysail   ("stay'sull") sail that is set on the stays running between the masts of a ship or from a mast to the deck. They are often triangular.

tackle   ("tay'kle") combination of ropes and pulleys used to hoist, lower, or trim sails.

topgallant mast   the third section of a mast.

topmast   the second section of a mast.

weighed anchor   lifted or raised the anchor in preparation for departure.

yardarms   the outermost sections of a yard, which can extend over the water. Royal Navy punishments were often performed from the yardarms.

yards   spars, or long wooden arms, that are horizontally suspended from the mast to carry sails.

young gentlemen   upper-class youths who by virtue of political connections are assigned to ships as apprentice officers.

SOURCE NOTES

I began unraveling John Ledyard's complicated life more than twelve years ago. What set me on the journey to write *Magnificent Voyage* was the discovery of correspondence and notes originally compiled in the early 1800s by an ambitious American clergyman named Jared Sparks. After years of research, Sparks published a best-selling (though inaccurate) biography, *The Life and Travels of John Ledyard*, in 1828. His notes and correspondence are housed at the Houghton Library, Harvard University.

I was fortunate to have access to John Ledyard's Russia journal and numerous letters to his family, which were provided to me by the Lorenzo Collection at the New York State Historic Site in Cazenovia, New York, and by Dartmouth College Library and Rauner Special Collections. His fascinating correspondence with Thomas Jefferson was uncovered in *The Papers of Thomas Jefferson*, edited by J. P. Boyd.

John Ledyard's family background was illuminated in a diary kept by Joshua Hepstead, his great-grandfather, which was published by the New London Historical Society. The Hartford Historical Society provided helpful insights about early Connecticut history, colonial news from the *Connecticut Courant*, and inscriptions from Ledyard family tombstones.

Most inspiring to me was the valiant, exhaustive research done by English writer J. C. Beaglehole in *The Journals of Captain James Cook on His Voyages of Discovery*. His biography of Cook and *The Voyage of the* Resolution *and* Discovery, *1776–1780* also contain a wealth of details.

A Journal of Captain Cook's Last Voyage to the Pacific Ocean and in Quest of a North-West Passage, between Asia & America, by John Ledyard, fascinated me. Of great help were footnotes provided in *John Ledyard's Journal of Captain Cook's Last Voyage*, edited by James Kenneth Munford. In addition to Ledyard's journal published in 1783, I drew upon Cook's log and the records of nine seamen aboard the *Resolution* and

Discovery. These "scribbling" voyagers included Surgeon William Anderson, Captain Charles Clerke, First Lieutenant John Gore, Second Lieutenant James King, Lieutenant James Burney, Midshipman George Gilbert, Surgeon's Assistant David Samwell, Second Lieutenant John Rickman, and Midshipman James Trevenen.

Cook's last voyage was well documented by artists as well. Drawings and paintings of people, animals, and plants were created by professional painter John Webber. Sketches were also done by Surgeon's Mate William Ellis and by James Clevely, carpenter on the *Resolution*, whose drawings were made into paintings by his brother, John, a professional draftsman. Maps and views (depicting how the land looked from sea) were ably drawn by William Bligh, Edward Riou, Henry Roberts, and William Edgar.

Many of the illustrations used in this book were taken from lithographs of Webber's drawings in a rare 1784 copy of *A Voyage to the Pacific Ocean Undertaken, by the Command of His Majesty, for Making Discoveries in the Northern Hemisphere* (3 vols. and *Atlas*, vols. 1, 2 and 3, published by Order of the Lord Commissioners of the Admiralty). Special thanks go to Russell Maylone and his staff in the Special Collections Department, Northwestern University Library, Evanston, Illinois, for assistance in reproducing these images.

Gratitude also goes to the farsighted vision and generosity of the Society of Children's Book Writers and Illustrators, who provided me with a work-in-progress grant for this book.

BIBLIOGRAPHY

LEDYARD FAMILY AND
EARLY CONNECTICUT HISTORY

Barbour, Lucius Barnes. *Families of Early Hartford, Connecticut*. Baltimore: Geneological Publishing Co., 1977.

Caulkins, Frances M. *Stone Records of Groton*. Norwich, Conn.: New London County Historical Society, 1903.

Ledyard, Bill. *History of Ledyard, Connecticut*. Norwich, Conn.: Bill Library Association, 1901.

Marx, Jennifer. *Pirates and Privateers of the Caribbean*. Malabar, Fla.: Krieger Publishing Co., 1992.

Press Association Compilers. *Ledyard-Cass Biographical Records*. New York: The Press Association, 1924.

Shaw, Cass Ledyard. *The Ledyard Family in America*. West Kennebunk, Maine: Phoenix Publishing, 1993.

Stark, Charles R. *Groton, Connecticut, 1705–1905*. Stonington, Conn.: Palmer Press, 1922.

JOHN LEDYARD

Adams, William Howard. *The Paris Years of Thomas Jefferson*. New Haven, Conn.: Yale University Press, 1997.

Auger, Helen. *Passage to Glory*. Garden City, N.Y.: Doubleday, 1946.

Halliday, E. M. "Captain Cook's American." *American Heritage,* December 1961, 60–87.

Jefferson, Thomas. *The Papers of Thomas Jefferson*. Edited by Julian P. Boyd. Princeton, N.J.: Princeton University Press, 1954.

Ledyard, John. *Journals Through Russia and Siberia, 1787–88. The Journal and Selected Letters*. Edited by Stephen Watrous. Madison, Wisc.: University of Wisconsin Press, 1966.

Munford, J. Kenneth. "Did John Ledyard Witness Captain Cook's Death?" *Pacific Northwest Quarterly* 54, no. 2 (April 1963): 75–78.

Sparks, Jared. *The Life of John Ledyard, the American Traveller*. Boston: Little and Brown, 1847.

MARINES, ROYAL NAVY, AND SEA LIFE

Baynham, Henry. *From the Lower Deck*. Barre, Mass.: Barre Publishers, 1970.

Harland, John. *Seamanship in the Age of Sail*. Annapolis, Maryland: Naval Institute Press, 1984.

Henningsen, Henning. *Crossing the Equator*. Translated from the Danish. Munksgaard, 1961.

Houlding, J. A. *Fit for Service: The Training of the British Navy, 1715–1795*. Oxford: Clarendon Press, 1981.

Kemp, Peter. *The British Sailor: A Social History of the Lower Deck*. London: J. M. Dent and Sons, 1970.

Lafflin, John. *Jack Tar: Story of the British Sailor*. London: Cassell & Co., 1969.

Masefield, John. *Sea Life in Nelson's Time*. London: Mehune & Co., 1905.

Rediker, Marcus. *Between the Devil and the Deep Blue Sea: Merchant Seamen, Pirates, and the Anglo-American Maritime World*. Cambridge: Cambridge University Press, 1987.

Villiers, Alan. *Men, Ships and the Sea*. Washington, D.C.: National Geographic Book Service, 1973.

HEALTH ISSUES/HISTORY OF SYPHILIS

McGrew, Roderick. *Encyclopedia of Medical History*. New York: McGraw Hill, 1985.

Walkowitz, Judith. *Prostitution and Victorian Society*. Cambridge: Cambridge University Press, 1980.

CAPTAIN JAMES COOK:
HIS LIFE AND VOYAGES

Beaglehole, J. C. *The Life of Captain James Cook*. Stanford, Calif.: Stanford University Press, 1974.

Cameron, Roderick. *The Golden Haze with Captain Cook in the South Pacific*. New York: World Publishing, 1964.

Conner, Daniel, and Lorraine Miller. *Master Mariner Captain James Cook and the Peoples of the Pacific*. Vancouver: Douglas & McIntyre, 1978.

Fisher, Robin, and Hugh Johnston. *Captain James Cook and His Times*. Seattle: University of Washington Press, 1979.

Hough, Richard. *The Last Voyage of Captain James Cook*. New York: William Morrow, 1979.

Obeyesekere, Gananath. *The Apotheosis of Captain Cook: European Mythmaking in the Pacific*. Princeton, N.J.: Princeton University Press, 1992.

Rienits, Rex and Thea. *The Voyages of Captain Cook*. London: Paul Hamlyn, 1968.

Vaughan, Thomas, and A. A. St. C. M. Murray-Oliver. *Captain Cook, R.N., the Resolute Mariner*. New York: William Morrow, 1979.

Warner, Oliver. *Captain Cook and the South Pacific*. New York: American Heritage Publishing, 1963.

PUBLISHED JOURNALS AND
CHARTS ABOUT COOK'S LAST VOYAGE

Beaglehole, J. C., ed. *The Journals of Captain James Cook on His Voyages of Discovery*. Cambridge: Cambridge University Press, 1967.

Burney, James. *A Chronological History of North-Eastern Voyages of Discovery*. London: Payne and Foss, 1819.

Ellis, William. *An Authentic Narrative of a Voyage Performed by Captain Cook and Captain Clerke in His Majesty's Ships "Resolution" and "Discovery."* Vols. 1 and 2. London, 1783. New York: DaCapo Press, 1969.

Gilbert, George. *Captain Cook's Final Voyage: Journal of Midshipman George Gilbert*. Edited by Christine Holmes. Honolulu: University of Hawaii Press, 1982.

Holmes, Sir Maurice. *Captain Cook and Hawaii: A Narrative by David Samwell*. San Francisco: David Magee, 1957.

Ledyard, John. *A Journal of Captain Cook's Last Voyage to the Pacific Ocean and in Quest of a North-West Passage, between Asia and America*. Chicago: Quadrangle Books, 1963.

[Rickman, John]. *An Authentic Narrative of a Voyage to the Pacific Ocean*. Philadelphia: Robert Bell, 1783.

Skelton, R. A., ed. *Charts and Views Drawn by Captain James Cook and His Officers*. Cambridge: Cambridge University Press for the Hakluyt Society, 1953.

GENERAL INFORMATION ABOUT THE LAST VOYAGE

Elbert, Samuel H., ed. *Hawaiian Antiquities and Folklore*. Honolulu: University of Hawaii Press, 1959.

Lehane, Brendan. *The Northwest Passage*. Morristown, N.J.: Time Life Books, 1981.

ILLUSTRATION CREDITS

NOTE ABOUT JOHN WEBBER'S SKETCHES

In the 1780s the technology did not exist that allowed publishers to directly reproduce the original skeches created by John Webber, the expedition's artist. To illustrate the official published account of the third voyage, the Admiralty selected sixty-one of Webber's numerous sketches to be made into engravings. An engraving is an image etched on a special metal plate that then can be coated with ink and impressed on paper to create multiple printed copies. Webber oversaw the work of the numerous engravers from London. The project took four years to complete.

These images were so popular, Webber created several more engravings and aquatints, or colored reproductions, from his sketches. This business proved to be a profitable venture for Webber, who sold his voyage artwork for publication or private purchase until his death in 1793.

Webber's work included in *Magnificent Voyage* is a sampling of the engraved images reproduced from a rare copy from the Special Collections Department of Northwestern University of *A Voyage to the Pacific Ocean*, published in 1784.

ILLUSTRATION CREDITS

The pictures in this book are from the following sources and used by permission:

Engravings and historical maps from *A Voyage to the Pacific Ocean*. Courtesy Charles Deering McCormick Library of Special Collections, Northwestern University, Evanston, Illinois: endpapers and pages x, 33, 38 (both pictures), 41, 50, 54, 55, 57, 60, 67, 73, 76, 83 (both pictures), 85, 88, 89, 90, 93, 96, 97, 100, 103, 104, 107, 109, 111 (both pictures), 115, 119, 121, 123, 124, 130, 132 (both pictures), 134, 138, 140, 143, 147, 150, 154, 156 (both pictures), 164, 183, 184, 185, 188, and 189

New maps and the diagram of a full-rigged ship are by Heather Saunders: pages xiv, 80, 92, and 222

Engravings, portraits, and photographs. Courtesy National Library of Australia: pages xviii (nla.pic-an7678295-1), 27 (pIC OBJ A40008304), 29 (NK9670), 67 (U2348), 68 (2816663), 71 (T2819), 87 (AN225760), 95 (AN2818058), 120 (to come), 160 (2292701), 166 (R3398), 169 (S8922), and 174 (T266)

Lithograph. Courtesy Rauner Special Collections Library, Dartmouth College: page 2 (Neg. 563)

Watercolors. Courtesy National Maritime Museum, Greenwich, London: page 6 (top, PW 4247), (bottom, PW 4967)

Miniature. Courtesy Hood Museum of Art, Dartmouth College, Hanover, New Hampshire commissioned by the Trustees of Dartmouth College, Hanover, New Hampshire: page 20 (P.793.2)

Captain John Gore portrait in oils 1780 by John Webber reprinted by kind permission of the Governor-General of New Zealand: page 144

Prints and photographs. Courtesy Library of Congress: pages 198 (LC-USZ62-75384), 201 (LC-USZ62-56773), 202 (LC-USZ62-70300), and 206 (LC-USZ62-17372)

Cataloging and negative numbers appear in parentheses.

INDEX

Page numbers in *italics* refer to illustrations.